THE HIGH SCHOOL PRINCIPALSHIP: LESSONS SELDOM TAUGHT, RARELY DISCUSSED

by William W. Johnson, Ph.D.

ISBN-10: 1482065991
ISBN-13: 9781482065992
Library of Congress Control Number: 2013902026
CreateSpace Independent Publishing Platform,
North Charleston, SC

PREFACE

This book presents information seldom, if ever, covered in any graduate course for the principalship. Degrees, certificates, or licenses in school administration involve studying the theoretical and reviewing the research but seldom, if ever, dealing with practical applications. This book aims to bridge at least some portions of that considerable gap.

Educators new to the principalship have much to learn and consider in a very compacted time frame.

- Who talks with them about the expectations and responsibilities they have accepted for a staff of 150 employees, 1500 students, and a physical plant worth thirty million dollars? No one.

- Who provides the new principal with suggestions and options for routine or emergency building communications? No one.

- Does any superior review possible arrangements or rearrangements of collateral duties for the building assistant principals? No.

- Do superiors inform the new principal of existing board of education policies and union agreements that need to be reviewed as soon as possible? No.

You get the idea. Help is not on the way. You were supposed to learn all that in your graduate studies. However, you were studying the theoretical and current research in the literature, not the practical and the applied.

What do principal candidates look and listen for so they have a better idea of what awaits them at a school they are seriously considering for employment? Are there keys to the successes or struggles of the potential school under consideration? If the new principal position is offered, what needs to be done as quickly as possible while the "honeymoon" is in play? What can wait?

Who can benefit from this book? Educators seriously considering leaving the classroom or other occupations within the school system to study and prepare for school administration will find this book very helpful. Building administrators currently serving as assistant principals will find the book stimulating and enlightening. Incumbent principals will benefit from reading this book by verifying, solidifying, or modifying their own ideas on the chapter subjects. Revisiting some of the practical and applied problems addressed in the book could prompt and motivate a principal to initiate changes.

The saying goes that if educators attend a workshop and come away with even one new idea that they can apply at their school, the time and effort was worth the expenditure. This book represents such an opportunity and one need not even leave the building.

DEDICATION

This book is dedicated to educators who are contemplating or training for the principalship as well as current principals on the job every day. I am inspired by your unselfish and caring commitment to the youth of America. I am in awe of the daunting responsibilities on your shoulders as you pursue an effective educational institution. My hope is that this book fulfills some portion of your professional needs and supplements the diverse demands on your career.

Acknowledgements

Sharon Johnson, Author and Science Educator, Louisville, Colorado, for her encouragement, editing skills, and advice.

Barbara Stayton, Student Teacher Supervisor, Portland, Oregon, and retired assistant principal, for her inspiration, editing, and support throughout the preparations for this book.

James Alexander, Attorney, Evanston, Illinois, for his lifelong support, direct assistance, and unconditional friendship.

The faculties at Woodstock High School, Woodstock, Illinois; Fort Lupton High School, Fort Lupton, Colorado; Centaurus High School, Lafayette, Colorado; and Monarch High School, Louisville, Colorado; for giving me insights into the principles of quality education.

ABOUT THE AUTHOR

William Warren Johnson received a Bachelor of Science in Liberal Arts and Sciences from the University of Illinois at Chicago, a Master of Science in Biological Sciences and General Science, and a Ph.D. in Education from the University of Illinois at Champaign-Urbana. Bill worked as a graduate assistant at the University of Illinois Bureau of Educational Research for three years while pursuing his doctorate degree. After teaching high school math and biology for one year in a suburb of Chicago, Bill entered three years of active duty with the United States Navy. He attended the Naval Aerospace Medical Institute for six months that included flight training. After graduating and receiving his wings, he was assigned to teach aerospace physiology at the Naval Aviation Schools Command, Naval Air Station, Pensacola, Florida. While on active duty he was awarded several personal citations including the Navy Achievement Medal for "...excellence in teaching, exceptional service, and dedication to his students..." Bill was also recognized as "Instructor of the Year" by his commanding officer, and he earned four separate command first-place awards for "Iron Man" competition in physical fitness from 1969 to 1972. Upon leaving active duty in 1972, Bill remained in the active Naval Reserve for a total of 38 years of military service. After completing his doctoral studies in 1975, Bill started his administrative public school career as assistant principal at Woodstock High School, Woodstock, Illinois. His first building principalship began in 1977 and brought him and his family to Weld County, Colorado. He served as principal of Fort Lupton High School for eight years before moving to Boulder County, Colorado. Bill was principal of Centaurus High School for twelve years, part of the Boulder County Public Schools, Boulder, Colorado. In 1997, Bill had the opportunity of a lifetime to open a new, comprehensive high school to serve the expanding public school student population in east Boulder County. Within one year, he opened Monarch High School that eventually served 1600+ students. Bill is currently retired after serving as an administrator in four high schools over a period of 30 years.

Bill has written articles for the *Journal of Mammalogy*, *Audubon Bulletin*, *Transactions of the Illinois Academy of Science*, *Conference Proceedings* at Colorado State University, *Naval Aviation Safety Review*, *Illinois Principal*, and *Life Sciences Safety Review*. He also wrote a complete instruction manual for the Chief of Naval Air Basic Training titled *Visual Illusions and Spatial Disorientation*.

TABLE OF CONTENTS

Introduction

The High School Principalship: Lessons Seldom Taught, Rarely Discussed is an introduction to subjects of study almost never dealt with elsewhere. It is written to address practical and applied problems present in every school in America, especially high schools. It is assumed by principal preparation programs that building principals learn about the issues in this book by gradual or unconscious assimilation, on-the-job experiences (positive and negative), and trial and error.

Chapter One: Board Policies

Observations about principal shortcomings and potential consequences involving board of education policies are presented. The notions of delegation and responsibility are assessed. The idea of a safety valve for personnel caught in unusual situations is introduced.

Chapter Two: Communications

The lifeblood of the principalship is communications. In this chapter parents and staff are given attention with an emphasis on the importance of the written medium. Neglected facts about communications in an emergency are compulsory reading for principals.

Chapter Three: School Safety

Recurrent but often-overlooked violations of school safety that have potential implications for property damage, injuries to occupants, or deaths are highlighted in this chapter. Specific spaces in the building, the gym and auditorium, are emphasized for special attention to breaches of safety.

Chapter Four: Open or Closed Campus?

The pros and cons of a closed high school campus are featured with possible compromises. Transitioning from an open to closed campus with parent controls is detailed.

Chapter Five: Extracurricular Activities

The neglected value and importance of after-school supervised sports, clubs, music, drama, and journalism are characterized as essential elements driving a quality high school. Participation rates bolster these assertions.

Chapter Six: Coaches, Sponsors, and School Climate

Positive school climate is reinforced and given a huge boost conditioned on the conduct and precedents set by building coaches and sponsors. The keys to success are linked to hiring and monitoring.

Chapter Seven: Hazing

The opportunity and responsibility to drastically reduce or eliminate hazing at school is set forth in this chapter.

Chapter Eight: Student Lockers

Learn how the arrangement, distribution, and control of student lockers significantly affect school climate, safety, and decorum.

Chapter Nine: Religion in the School

A nationally recognized, well written, and accessible Board of Education Policy on the subject of religion in the schools is spotlighted in this chapter. The defensible position for principals is presented.

Chapter Ten: Personnel Evaluations

The principal's responsibility and delegating authority are underlined with recommendations for on-time, in-good-order task completion. Decisions regarding retention or non-retention of personnel are presented as the foundation for a quality school.

Chapter Eleven: Union Contracts

The role and responsibilities of the principal who works under one or more union contracts are the focus of this section. Pitfalls awaiting the principal are discussed.

Chapter Twelve: Student Publications

Both school-sponsored and non-school sponsored student publications are the topics of this chapter. Current trends in school-sponsored student publications warrant principal consideration.

Chapter Thirteen: Copying Machines

Principals are encouraged to attend to issues surrounding the irascible, indispensible, and mandatory copy machine(s). Copying access privileges are discussed for principal review.

Chapter Fourteen: The Assistant Principalship

An argument is made that the principal should reconsider the primary and collateral job duties and responsibilities for assistant principals. Specialized AP job assignments are viewed as counterproductive for both the institution and the individual.

Chapter Fifteen: Curriculum

Getting new personnel acquainted with their assigned teaching courses is addressed in this chapter. Controversial courses, required readings, deviations from the prescribed curriculum, and teacher course selection for the following school year also receive attention.

Chapter Sixteen: Governance

The convoluted challenges and potential rewards involving building governance are appraised. Elements that should be considered in organizing or reorganizing building governance are assessed.

Chapter Seventeen: The Single High School District vs. Districts with Multiple High Schools

Current or future principals will gain insights into key differences between single and multiple high school districts that will aid personal decision making if a change is under consideration.

Chapter Eighteen: Student Activity Fund

The seemingly innocuous and modest tasks and responsibilities surrounding the student activity fund are spotlighted in this chapter. Handling cash in a school setting receives emphasis.

Chapter Nineteen: More Changes for School Improvement

The traditional school letter awarded for extracurricular activities is reviewed with suggestions for expansion and revisions. Student daily class attendance problems receive a major change for improvement. Student seat time is discussed.

Chapter Twenty: A Model to Address Principal Responsibilities

The 1954 writings of Abraham Maslow are presented as a model for principals to view their school and their responsibilities to enhance student esteem and self-actualization.

Addendum: Opening a New High School

Any principal given the rare opportunity to open a new high school will benefit from reading this chapter about the experiences and insights of five experienced principals who planned and opened new buildings. Unexpected pitfalls are highlighted.

Chapter 1

BOARD POLICIES - THE RULES AND REGULATIONS FOR RUNNING A SCHOOL

INTRODUCTION

Every school district in the United States maintains a set of detailed and written policies, regulations, and rules pertaining to every aspect of the operation of the schools within the district. It is the duty and responsibility of the local board of education in each school district to review, oversee, revise, execute, and maintain these policies, regulations, and rules of operation.

Examples of chapters in many board of education policies include:

- Foundations and Basic Commitments

- Board Governance and Operations

- General School Administration

- Fiscal Management

- Support Services

- Facilities Development

- Personnel

- Negotiations

- Instruction

- Students

- School-Community Relations

- Education-Agency Relations

The good news about school board policies is that in most large school districts they are now online. Years ago a principal had to travel to the district offices to view the volumes of written policies each of which were inches thick with an index that was of limited help in finding anything inside. Today you can access the district policies online, 24/7, from any computer with wonderful search engine assistance.

KEEP YOUR JOB

One of the most frustrating events for members of the local school board and the superintendent of schools is having problematic information placed in front of them clearly indicating that a building principal has failed to recognize, observe, or execute one or more written school board policies. Both the school board and superintendent are by nature, with rare exception, supportive of their schools and their building principals. Both are also equally distressed and agitated when they have to rule against or fail to support a principal due to failure to carry out the written rules and directives (school board policies) of the district.

Failure to execute board of education policies, either out of ignorance or with malice, is one of the top reasons for the dismissal, demotion, or resignation of a principal.

Fortunately, the solution for this dilemma is relatively simple. Read, digest, and carry out the written policies of the board of education. When in doubt about "grey areas" of the policies and directives, ask your immediate supervisor for an interpretation as applied to the situation you are confronted with and investigating.

In your personal notes, record the date, time, person you talked to about the application of the board policy, and the advice given. If you were passed off to another person up or down the chain of command, record that as well. You get the idea.

DELEGATION AND RESPONSIBILITY

Please remember that you can, should, and must delegate authority to your subordinates, but never forget that you retain responsibility and accountability for their actions. However, you can dampen potential negative effects reflecting on you resulting from any unfortunate and misguided actions or deeds performed by subordinates. You may need to demonstrate that you were both timely and prudent in instilling the rules and policies of the board of education to these same subordinates. Keep track of your work with dates, times, actions, and events in your personal notes.

A systematic approach to introducing board of education policies to subordinates, primarily assistant principals, can be a daunting task considering the volume of material involved. I recommend starting with the section or chapter on student discipline followed by policies on daily attendance, residence, and attendance areas. Establish calendar dates during the school year linked to chapters or sections of the board policies for study and review with your subordinates. Some sections will result in a light skim and others will warrant in-depth scrutiny. I cannot emphasize enough how time spent on this endeavor will return substantial benefits to the overall administration and daily conduct of the school as well as the principal's personal reputation and status. The time saved backtracking on the misapplication of board policies alone justifies the time spent on the activity.

I highly recommend parallel study of the union or meet-and-confer agreements for all employee groups. There was always something uncanny about the constant feeling that I knew the teachers' contract better than the union members. On a related note, never hesitate to call the union or union officials with questions about specific sections of the contract. Seek their interpretation and application. You need not share your local issue as you ask for interpretations if it is not in your best interest. Attempt to maintain cordial relations at all times during an inquiry. If you encounter hostilities or hostile attitudes from a simple inquiry, politely disengage and contact your immediate superior with the same question(s).

THE SAFETY VALVE

While it is true that you desire subordinates who emanate confidence and assertiveness, you can limit errors in judgment and having to backtrack on those errors by clearly establishing what might be called safety valves. Subordinates need to know that you invite and appreciate interruptions of your day to review and discuss situations and decisions they are anticipating. Competent assistant principals understand the fine line between "I need help and advice with this situation and decision," verses "I know what to do and what's right, but I don't want to or can't do it." The safety valve that you have given them is not only permission but also an expectation that they stop or stabilize a situation in the school long enough to seek help, advice, and/or assistance.

Instances ripe for employing a safety valve could include:

- An encounter with an unfamiliar discipline situation or violation not clearly covered by a current school rule.

- An escalating student/parent anger situation.

- Another discipline incident involving a chronic offender.

- Student/parent accusations regarding staff members.

- Previous negative history with a student/parent.

- Incidents by or involving special education students.

- An incident likely to require involvement of authorities outside the school (police).

- Information provided by a student that exceeds the authority or sphere of influence of assistant principal's actions.

In most situations, competent assistant principals will also begin to consult board policies and rules on their own when confronted by new, unusual, or unfamiliar issues of student discipline, attendance, or other job-related questions. This will be a clear indicator of job growth and improved understanding of the expectations, roles, and responsibilities of the assistant principalship that will transfer to a principalship.

This same discussion regarding the use of a safety valve also applies to all personnel in your building. All school personnel should have the safety valve in their personal repertoire of interactive skills for use with students, parents, and other staff members. A verbal tool to defuse and disarm an escalating or potentially explosive interaction in the classroom, hallway, or other educational setting is essential for a more positive school climate. The technique of inserting a time delay with appropriate recognition of a complaint is a safety valve worthy of a staff development session at your school. Empower your faculty and staff members.

—∿—

Chapter 2

Communications

Introduction

The number one challenge to the contemporary building principal is communications. How exactly can principals connect with and influence literally thousands of individuals under their umbrella? A large high school of say 1600 students will have about 3200 parents, approximately 150 staff members on the payroll, and potentially hundreds of unpaid volunteers. These numbers will remain roughly proportional as the size of the school goes up or down from 1600.

The smaller the high school the closer the principal can remain to the student population in terms of daily interactions, knowledge of parents and relatives, and direct personal influence on that population. As student numbers increase, several things happen.

- Numbers of personnel increase - more teachers, assistant principals, security, department heads, counselors, paraprofessionals, and secretaries.

- Numbers of curricular and extracurricular programs increase.

- Complexity of the institution increases exponentially.

- Principal distance from the students increases.

Direct, hands-on management of larger numbers gives way to indirect management through mechanisms of written and more selective verbal communications. Department heads and assistant principals assume leadership roles in larger high schools. How does a principal:

- Assert leadership throughout the school year?

- Prevent or reduce the filtering of information or the spreading of rumors?

- Maintain clarity, transparency, direction, and access?

- Get and keep a school moving towards its prime directives?

COMMUNICATIONS WITH STAFF

My most important communication tool was the "Monday Morning Memo." On the first day of most weeks throughout the school year, I provided staff members with both official and unofficial information about education, the district, and the building. I also sprinkled in my own opinions on selected topics from time to time. I asked staff members to read my Monday Morning Memo (MMM) to keep their calendars filled with important dates and events, their heads filled with data, and their hearts focused on their students. I gave everyone both a hard copy of the MMM in their official building mailbox in the main administrative office and an electronic copy for those on the operational building email list. Experience has shown that issuing both the electronic and hard copies are necessary to meet the preferred learning styles of staff members and the multiple uses to which the MMM is put.

Reviewing only my past eight school years as a principal, I dissected and classified the entries in my 288 Monday Morning Memos under 53 topics dealing with every aspect of school life and every ingredient that constitutes a high functioning, comprehensive, American public high school.

I am convinced that a high quality, well thought out, articulate, open, and honestly written weekly document is the primary vehicle to lead, guide, and positively influence your school. I hasten to add that you must pay special attention to proper spelling and grammar.

Professionals working in concert on a common set of agreed upon prime directives need a concrete, sustained, and targeted written document focused on the institution.

- Substance is provided to agree with, argue about, think about, or reflect on.

- All employees are given goals and challenged to work together.

- Data are provided from the past giving hope and direction for the future.

- Accomplishments of both the staff and students are highlighted.

- Dirty laundry is put in writing for all to view and address as necessary.

- Rumors are neutralized.

- Notices of dates and deadlines keep the complex institution more efficient.

- School policies, rules, and practices are reinforced.

- Warnings and cautions are put in writing for all to assimilate.

- Details from all corners of the complex school are made common knowledge to all staff members.

- Achievement is celebrated across the full spectrum of the school.

- No single program, department, or person is featured at the expense of others.

- The rare quality of personalization is renewed.

- Expectations for staff and faculty conduct and performance are consistently put in writing.

- The principal's leadership is featured and expressed throughout the school year.

- This weekly document has the net effect of:

  ○ Expanding collegiality.

  ○ Bringing staff members closer together.

  ○ Reducing the isolation so common in large institutions.

  ○ Improving positive school climate and overall school safety.

  ○ Stimulating staff and faculty communications.

  ○ Improving and sustaining staff and faculty morale and motivation.

FACULTY AND STAFF MEETINGS

I found it helpful to break building personnel meetings into separate faculty and support staff meetings. It is advantageous to further divide support staff meetings into groups by job specialty such as custodians, secretaries, security team members, lunchroom workers, paraprofessionals, and in-season head coaches of sports teams. At all meetings it is essential that you provide an outline of agenda items, hopefully before the meeting if at all possible. At the start of a meeting, you can call for additional agenda items from the members present. Near the end of faculty or staff meetings, it is often prudent to ask the group if anyone present wishes to address the meeting with any announcements, points of interest, and upcoming events that need emphasis.

The problem with most high school faculty meetings centers on the after-school obligations and programs that pervade the weekly schedule. Literally hundreds and hundreds of high school students remain after school dismissal for the day to participate in sports and non-sports activities. This creates the dilemma of forcing significant numbers of teachers to attend faculty meetings while throngs of students mill about unsupervised waiting for their coaches and sponsors to connect with them. The potential lack of adult supervision is unacceptable. On the other hand, an all-faculty meeting without the entire faculty is an exercise in futility.

I have unsuccessfully tried holding two faculty meetings in a day with members being invited and required to attend one before school or the traditional meeting after school. Interestingly, the faculty resisted this option with many members saying they thought it was counterproductive to conduct such meetings with so many members missing (because they were at the earlier/later meeting).

Perhaps it was that school, that faculty, a general lack of interest in all-faculty meetings, or my skills and abilities that failed to make those meetings worthwhile.

The best solution to getting all-faculty members together at one time and in one space occurred when I was able to carve out time during the regular school day in a space large enough to hold everyone. All-faculty meetings were held at least once a month and more frequently as needed. The meeting time was tied to a change in the weekly school schedule that we called "late start." One day a week school started for students at 9:30 a.m. instead of 7:30 a.m. During this two-hour period, a variety of necessary and helpful meetings were established including all-faculty meetings, department meetings, and building committee meetings (not all on the same day!).

Most meetings lasted a maximum of one hour, so "tutor time" was designated for the second hour allowing teachers to conduct one-on-one help sessions with struggling students or small groups of students. Extracurricular practices or meetings were not permitted during this time. I never had a teacher tell me that they were idle during "tutor time" because all of their students were doing just fine.

One unexpected and very positive outcome of employing the weekly late start program was improved school climate. High school faculty members really liked and appreciated meeting on school time at the beginning of the school day. They were fresh, alert, focused, and attentive at 7:30 a.m. and not tired and exhausted, as was often the case at 3:15 p.m. On late-start days when building committee meetings, department meetings, and/or student tutor times occurred, faculty members expressed greater satisfaction with the conduct and achievements of the activities.

HEAD-COACH MEETINGS

The best arrangement I've experienced for meeting with head coaches is before the start of school in the fall and then once a month, usually at 6:30 a.m., with an additional meeting if something comes up that cannot wait for the regularly scheduled monthly meeting. Providing refreshments is money well spent but just be sure the expenditure is legal and ethical if taken from building funds. If it is not, dig in your own pocket.

The role of the principal at head-coach meetings is not to usurp the duties and responsibilities of the athletic director (AD) but rather to set the tone for coach leadership expectations, personal coach conduct, and duties involving assistant coaches and volunteers. Expectations for coach interactions with players and parents should be made clear. Safety valves for the coach in difficult situations should be offered and discussed. (Presented in Chapter One.)

After the initial meeting in the fall, the principal should consider a drop-in role for the monthly meetings. Monitoring the athletic director in action is an important leadership function as well as gathering data for the AD's annual personnel evaluation.

COMMUNICATIONS WITH PARENTS

Opportunities for communications with parents are plentiful and varied. Parent-teacher conferences create special one-on-one occasions between individual classroom teachers and parents/guardians to focus on and discuss their student. One complaint high school parents have regarding parent-teacher conferences is the frustration generated by chasing up/down and all over the school trying to locate teachers only to find a long line of fellow parents waiting to see the same teacher. Some high schools have had success with scheduling appointments with teachers. I am one who has not had satisfactory results with appointments. My "solution" to this quandary is to eliminate appointments and move lunchroom tables into the gym(s) and seat teachers by department with large overhead signs identifying them and their location.

Lines still form but parents can see available teachers and move to the shortest wait. The running around the building frustration marathon is eliminated. Counselors and administrators are also in the gyms and visible for personal contacts and informal conversations. The limited numbers of teachers not at conferences, for whatever reasons, leave sign-up sheets at their department location. Parents leave them notes and requests for phone contacts that are fulfilled in the next few school days or evenings. One spinoff benefit of this large, single space approach to parent-teacher conferences allows parents to make visual connections with all members of the staff by department as well as connecting with other parents.

13

After-hours activity programs also give parents special opportunities to connect with sports coaches and non-sports activity coaches and sponsors. A large high school usually offers:

- Over twenty-five sports teams for men and women.

- A variety of band programs.

- Several choirs.

- Orchestra.

- Speech and debate.

- Media groups such as yearbook and newspapers.

- Student government.

- Class representatives.

- Vocational teams and clubs.

- Spirit squads and dance teams.

- Technology teams and competitions.

- Drama and theatre.

- An abundance of high interest clubs.

All school personnel in these wonderful after-school activities should be encouraged, perhaps required, to create time and opportunity for parent visits and observe their students in action. One or more parent opportunities to meet and communicate with the coach/sponsor should also be planned at a convenient time and place for parents.

A monthly direct mail or email (or both) parent newsletter is traditional in American high schools and still holds favorable interest among today's parents. While this is a one-way communication vehicle, it does provide an excellent opportunity for a school to put its best foot forward and feature the incredible achievements of staff and students. School calendars with deadline reminders are very popular.

The most current and helpful direct communication with parents and guardians is the electronic media. Messages can be delivered very quickly from the principal regarding emergencies, rumors that need explanation, and reminders of last minute changes to previously published schedules based on weather problems and other unforeseeable complications.

COMMUNICATIONS WITH SUPERVISORS

As a courtesy to your immediate supervisor, you should consider sending them a copy of your written communications to your staff. Keeping your supervisor informed regarding the events and happenings at the school can be the basis for improving trust and a positive relationship. How the supervisor deals with the steady stream of information may be different.

Most supervisors I worked with accepted the weekly information with interest. Their comfort level with my open communications seemed to lower any concerns and stress levels they might have had regarding my day-to-day conduct and management of the building. Occasionally, the information served as a stimulus for quality conversations between us. Trust levels between us improved and barriers to honest, open communications were lowered. The school was the ultimate benefactor.

However, over the years, one supervisor elected to use the weekly written copy of my communications with the building staff to micromanage. Each week's memo caused almost immediate phone calls demanding explanations. This included a streak of criticism over specific items in the memo and unsolicited advice on, not only my style of working with the building staff, but also how things should be handled in the future. I instinctively stopped sending this supervisor a copy of the memos. Interestingly, he never contacted me to ask why they stopped. He never demanded that they continue. In short, I never heard from him on the topic again, and to this day, I have no idea why. I do know that he departed the district at the end of that school year. (I am not implying a connection with my communication device.)

COMMUNICATIONS IN EMERGENCIES

What about communications under high states of emergency? Do not wait for an emergency to learn by experience what works and what fails in the worst-case scenarios at your building. Take the examples given here and verify your status should you ever need to take charge and respond. These are high stakes issues for you and your school. Be sure your assistant principals are informed and aware of the issues. Practice your responses, and be sure your equipment is functional.

In the event of total power failure, what electrical backup do you have for the building-wide public address system? The first time I experienced a catastrophic loss of electricity, the PA system did not function. I could not talk to the staff and/or students. Interior rooms with no windows were totally dark. Teachers quickly lost control of enough students to be problematic for all. My running through the halls with a hand-held loud speaker was a joke of monumental proportions.

The school had a back-up generator. I discovered that the back-up generator was only attached to the building's fire light fixtures and exit signs. So, about every tenth ceiling light in the main halls was lit. One light in the ceiling of the gym was lit. No power to the building PA system. No communications with students and staff. To make things even more interesting, the deputy superintendent informed me during this power loss that I was to keep the school in session. No early release, no busses. We survived, but what if we lost power with the addition of a fire, structural failure, or worse yet, an armed intruder?

At my next school, new and modern by all standards, I immediately investigated what the automatically activated standby generator would support in the event of a loss of power to the building. Much to my chagrin, I discovered that the building-wide public address system was not wired to the back-up generator. In addition, the pump system needed to lift raw sewage away from the campus to the treatment plant was also not supported by a back-up generator.

During a subsequent actual power outage, the sewage pump became inoperable causing the entire lower level under the gym containing the locker rooms, offices, and weight rooms to be inundated with eight inches of raw stinking sewage. Within six months, a second, more powerful automatic stand-by electrical generator was purchased, installed, and attached to the lift station and building PA system.

Let's talk about cell phones in an emergency at school. If there is a lock down at a high school with an enrollment of 1600 students that is announced over the public address system, you can be certain that about 1600 cell phone calls will be attempted within minutes of the announcement. You must make the all-school public address announcement, no question. The potential problem for building administrators dependent on cell phone communications themselves is a failure of the cell phone system due to local overload. If students decide to text rather than call, the affect may not be as devastating. The surefire solution could depend on having one fail-proof phone (land line) in a secure location in the building guaranteed to connect an administrator directly to the outside world (police, fire, and/or district offices) regardless of the anomalies and complications of the ongoing emergency.

High schools employing and depending on a feature with cell phones called "push-to-talk" for person-to-person communications among building administrators, security personnel, and custodians could also experience a loss of service due to the overload scenario described above. Hand-held, two-way communicators would not be affected by a loss of cell phone service but they seldom have a range beyond the immediate building. Normal building landlines would also be unavailable as staff members occupy all the lines with their personal calls out of the building. The volume of incoming calls from the community would also render regular landlines unavailable for administrative use regarding the ongoing emergency. A dedicated, protected, and secure single landline is recommended to address this serious problem.

It would be wise to have a copy of board of education policy directives handy to grab at a moments notice of an emergency. Having immediate access to the names and numbers of persons cited in the policies would facilitate and accelerate proper execution of the directives.

—⁓—

Chapter 3

SCHOOL SAFETY

INTRODUCTION

My purpose is not to cover every contingency imaginable under the topic of safety in our schools. Instead, I will highlight a few experiences I have had that seem to pass under the radar of many K-12 school principals. Taking note of these common issues of safety lapses could prevent a catastrophe in your school and community.

HOLIDAY DECORATIONS–LIVE TREE MATERIALS

Let me start with holiday decorations. It should be made clear and enforced that no live tree materials may be brought into the schoolhouse. This includes garlands. No amount of daily watering or "fire proofing" can significantly reduce the explosive fireball produced by the accidental or intentional ignition of cut evergreen materials. Seasonal student sales of trees and garlands for fundraising should also be banned from inside the building, even overnight. You could offer an outside, detached storage building as a temporary alternative to using the main building.

GASOLINE MOTOR STORAGE

Most schools will have a custodian, vocational teacher, or technology teacher that stores a gas-powered machine or two inside the school. Machines might include lawnmowers, edge trimmers, bush trimmers, pumps, generators, snow blowers, chain saws, sport-field lining machines, golf carts, and other on-site transportation vehicles. The principal must find space for gasoline motor storage outside and detached from the main school building and ensure enforcement. The trusty snow blower cannot be stored inside the main school building even overnight so that it will be toasty and start without hassles on a cold winter morning. Storage of gas cans inside the school building must also be prohibited.

DOORS AND UNAUTHORIZED SCHOOL ENTRY

Here is a simple recommendation: Do not ever allow "chaining" of school doors, inside or outside, weekdays, weekends, vacation times, or summer breaks. Eliminating the potential injury or loss of life possible under the practice of chaining supersedes unauthorized entry, vandalism, or theft. It could even be the unsavory thief or student vandals who die when trapped in a hallway with a chained exit after they set a fire behind them to cover their deed. Life trumps property.

Unauthorized persons may gain entry into schools because the mullion (the part of the door frame between the double doors) flexes enough to "pop" the locked doors open. A pry bar or two-by-four does the job. Some locked older doors are loose enough that they can be "jerked" open by a sturdy individual.

I have a fix for this dilemma. Remove the handles on many, if not all, of these outside doors not including main entrances. The common "C" door handle gives the offender an excellent leverage location to pry the door open or a good hand hold for the more muscular intruder. A round knob-type door handle on the outside is better in terms of providing a less useful grip, but it is still an attractive and sometimes valuable traction point. It is very difficult to pry or pull open a heavy metal fire door with nothing to grasp. With an occasional exception, the key inserted into the lock is sufficient to allow opening and entry by authorized personnel. For main door entrances that must have a handle, consider removing one of the two "C" handles per set of double doors.

As an extra incentive to protect your staff and students, consider the consequences of a deliberate or thoughtless stunt by the disabling of a double "C" handle set of exit doors. This is done by the simple act of sliding a two-by-four through the two "C" handles and then setting off the fire alarm. An even more sinister action would involve doing the same thing with chain and padlock. As stated above, removing even one of the two "C" handles on a double entry/ exit door would go a long way toward eliminating this threat.

I recommend this same alteration for double gym doors that exit into adjoining hallways inside the school. Some teenage minds might devise a "prank" involving two-by-fours through all the double gym doors with "C" handles during an all-school assembly or evening sports event followed by a false fire alarm. Panic is the primary cause of injury and death in this scenario. You really only need one "C" handle to open, unlock, or enter a set of double exit gym doors. If you really need two handles, come up with something other than the vandal-friendly "C" handles.

AUDITORIUM SAFETY

The auditorium of most public schools has a number of safety issues that remain unnoticed and uncorrected especially during performances. Let's start with those schools lucky enough to have an orchestra pit. Sometimes the pit has a hard cover that is only removed for performances and practices leading up to the performances. An orchestra pit must have a safety net installed anytime the pit is uncovered. A cargo net or the relatively inexpensive netting used for batting cages by your softball/baseball teams will do the job. Visualize one of your students falling ten to twenty feet onto a concrete slab in the pit that usually has music stands and chairs covering the area. This is a great motivator to get the job done. By the way, you can always fashion a "hole" in the netting to allow the orchestra leader to observe cues on stage.

Auditoriums have fixed furniture for more than one reason. In the event of an emergency, real or perceived, you do not want loose furniture present that can become jammed into the exits thus limiting or prohibiting the rapid, unrestricted egress of patrons. It did not matter how many times and in how many schools I have harped on this issue with drama, theatre, and music staff members; I would still find tables, chairs, props, decorations, and set designs at or near room exits with performances only days, or even worse, hours away. On occasion, decorations were deliberately placed to hide a double exit doorway or block the light from overhead doorway exit signs or isle lights because "they might distract from the performance."

My advice is that you or your supervising representative must monitor these "last minute" issues days before a performance and, again, hours before a performance. Just before patrons are admitted to a performance, you must also literally test all exit doors to be sure they open freely as designed with nothing on the outside of the door prohibiting or restricting full movement. Snow (outside doors that open to the exterior of the building), furniture, stacked boxes, musical instruments, props, or scenery to be used in a performance are often culprits. Never allow overflow or standing-room-only crowds to fetch folding chairs to be placed at the sides, front, rear, or in aisles around the auditorium.

Wheelchairs placed on the ends of rows of fixed seating or in the aisles can create the same hazards as unfixed seating like folding chairs, tables, or other loose furniture. If you do not have specific spaces for wheelchairs, have a small section of fixed seats removed to create the space and enforce their use.

Regular auditorium inspections should include a checklist of items like the following that each school can embellish as needed:

- Replace burned out lights in the ceiling, exit signs, and small aisle markers.

- Replace or repair torn carpet and other potential trip hazards.

- Doors not leading to a legal exit (doors leading to storage rooms) should have a substantial sign posted on them stating "not an exit."

- Adequate fire extinguishing equipment in place.

- Safety wires in place anchoring all performance-related light fixtures attached to pipe bars.

Students should not be allowed on overhead catwalks during performances. An announcement should be made to patrons before every performance pointing out emergency exits and procedures in the unlikely event of an unexpected problem. This is critical for audiences containing adults not familiar with the building.

Beware of unauthorized curtains showing up as loans or donations. They usually will not meet the standards of fireproofing required for schools. Donated furniture for the auditorium may not be sturdy enough for school use. Homemade props should undergo scrutiny. Fresh cut evergreen trees and garnishes should never be allowed in the building. Live fire such as candles on sets should never be allowed. Anything resembling high wire or overhead lifts, trap door equipment, and pyrotechnics should send shivers up and down your body and be found inappropriate for the high school setting no matter how long and loud students or the drama teacher argue.

Assess your stagecraft area. Power tools can be very dangerous in the hands of unsupervised teenagers. Paints and solvents must be properly stored and vented at all times. Rags and cleanup materials require special handling. The local fire marshal can perform a safety assessment for you. Avoid the urge to save too much from one set construction event to the next. Saving money is prudent, but storing so much that you cannot safely turn around in the storage space is foolhardy.

GYM SAFETY

If you do not have extra time and money to make specialized repairs, take note. Do not allow physical education teachers and coaches who use the gym to allow students to have the keys to operate the mat lift, divider curtain, bleachers extractor, audio equipment, or basketball backboard lifts.

Do not allow custodians to save time and cut corners by not setting up the railing equipment on the ends of seating bleachers or those used as aisle railings. When someone falls off the end of a bleacher during a basketball game or trips going up or down an aisle, the authorities will be looking for the principal, not the custodian.

On more than one occasion, I have entered the gym just prior to an event hosting well over a thousand spectators only to observe two of the four double-door corner exits from the gym completely blocked. The band and performers' equipment and paraphernalia completely took up the spaces in front of half of the emergency exit doors. Do not allow the band or other performing groups to block any exit doors or isles with equipment that would prohibit the orderly egress of people from the gym in the event of a real or perceived emergency.

When dismissing students from an all-school assembly in the gym, do so by class or section seating. This will minimize the very real possibility that students who fail to understand the potential for serious injury will start pushing those in front of them given the anonymity of the mass exodus. I have seen students go down in this scenario with resulting injuries. Special education students are particularly vulnerable. Dismiss roughly a fourth at a time and keep the others seated using faculty help as necessary. Dismissing seniors first followed by juniors, sophomores, and then freshmen is an excellent sequence to maintain orderliness and safety.

SNOW REMOVAL

One of the most common and potentially serious safety problems germane to schools in snow zones is the failure of the custodial staff to remove ice and snow piled up outside the building blocking exit doors. Now I'm not talking necessarily about the main entrance/exit doors. They're obvious. They're used when school is open, and they get cleared when it snows. I'm referring to those exit doors almost never used by staff and student foot traffic. They're in unusual locations like at the end of seldom-used hallways, just off specialized spaces like the auditorium or music rooms, where architectural school fire laws require them and teachers never let students routinely use them.

After getting to work extra early on a particularly snowy winter school day, custodians or district maintenance workers promptly and efficiently clear snow from all the normal outside spaces. Now exhausted and inside to rest, warm up, and get on with the days regular responsibilities, guess which doors still have a six-foot wind-blown drift completely blocking them? It's your responsibility to have the problem checked and corrected, and you won't be popular when you do.

FIRE DOORS

It is a good idea to ensure that staff and faculty members understand the concept of the hallway fire doors used throughout your school. Most of those doors are held open by electromagnets that automatically release the doors to close during the activation of the fire alarm system. Primary purposes of the location of these fire doors are to prevent the spread of flames, and perhaps more importantly, the spread of smoke throughout the school in a real fire situation. Fire doors are constructed to be big, thick, heavy, and hunky to withstand intense heat for many hours before failing.

Disabling or blocking these fire doors from assuming their shut-tight position in an emergency is tantamount to placing unknown numbers of students and staff in harms way. Opening the fire doors once they have slammed shut is contraindicated, foolish, dangerous, and, perhaps, criminal. Required monthly all-school fire drills must emphasize these facts as well as pointing out that the proper direction to egress is out the nearest unblocked exit. Teachers are the key to assessing the situation at their location in the school and directing students to the appropriate exit(s). Principals must discuss these "mundane" issues with all staff members.

PAPER ON HALL LOCKERS, CEILINGS, AND WALLS

Think about the amount of paper, flammable paper, that adorns student hall lockers celebrating birthdays, holidays, and students running in school elections. In addition, wall posters announcing upcoming dances and other student events can approach huge proportions unless restricted by rules. Sometimes paper signage is stretched overhead across hallways for maximum visual effect. One unclear thinker with a Bic lighter can turn decorations into flames in seconds. Smoke and panic could cause more injuries than the flames.

Imagine that as you arrive to supervise a homecoming dance in the main gym, you observe the main hallway leading to and from the gym to the lunchroom completely lined, sides and ceiling, with paper. Brought-from-home tree lights were also strung among the paper decorations everywhere imaginable. Regular hall ceiling lights were completely sealed off with decorations to create ambience. Students had worked all day preparing the festivities. Over a thousand students subsequently attended.

Did you properly brief the faculty sponsor(s) ahead of time on the limits to paper, strings of lights, and decorations/props, especially those brought from home? Did you immediately check to see if all emergency exits were free and clear for the egress of participants if needed? Were emergency lights uncovered and visible? Did the band or DJ hired intend to use pyrotechnics or fogging equipment?

While limiting the sizes, locations, and materials used in this example, you should also consider rules prohibiting the posting of signage on the glass in hall, exit, and classroom doors. Glass in the doors was designed to allow people to see someone coming on the other side of the door. Avoid injuries--don't allow door windows to be covered. Blocking the windows with signage eliminates the purpose of the glass.

LOOSE FURNITURE

It should be made clear that issues I raised about tables, chairs, and other loose (unfixed) furniture in the auditorium also apply to other spaces in the school. In a vocational shop for example, wood and other rare materials to be used in student projects cannot be stacked and stored in such a manner that exit doors are blocked. Art rooms, band and choir rooms, stagecraft spaces, and any rooms with an extra exit door may not be blocked for any reason. Based on my experiences, I must unfortunately add that the principal must constantly monitor this potential problem.

I have seen at least one high school where students requested and were given lounge-type furniture, tables, and chairs in the main halls of the building. One of the areas may even have been designated a senior lounge. I do not recall. What struck me was the safety issue occurring during a mass exodus of the building during a real or perceived emergency usually prompted by the building fire alarm. School architects set the number and width of hallways and the number and locations of exit doors and stairways based on maximum flow patterns of people exiting the various parts of a school building during an emergency. Restricting the usable space of such hallways, exits, and stairways in an emergency egress with the imposition of loose furniture and equipment creates unplanned barriers and sets the stage for a catastrophe.

Hallways, exits, and stairways in a school must be kept clear and free at all times when students are present. It is the principal's responsibility.

SCIENCE LABS

Don't wait for the local fire marshal or OSHA (Occupational Safety and Health Administration) representative to perform an impromptu inspection of your science classrooms before you ensure that they are in conformance with common sense safety guidelines as well as national and state standards. (Note: You can obtain excellent help from science supply companies like Finn Scientific.)

- All lab equipment must be in good working order.

- Ventilated hoods must be operational and used when appropriate.

- Eyewashes and safety showers should be operationally tested regularly.

- Student safety equipment, such as eye protection, must be clean and operational.

- Chemicals must be stored in a ventilated and locked storage cabinet or room.

- Disposal of chemicals must follow strict safety standards.

- Chemical shelf-life limits must be monitored and honored.

- Up-to-date lists of chemicals must be kept in the science and principal's offices.

- Provisions for the proper disposal of biological materials and animal parts from dissections must be in place.

Fellow staff members will also greatly appreciate timely notification of laboratory experiments being conducted in science spaces that produce odors, offensive or pleasant. All science teachers must have information and instructions on the protocols for spillage, injuries, glass breakage, and chemical hazards.

The principal should make it clear to all science teachers that certain chemical reactions in the schoolhouse are forbidden. The thermite reaction is a good example. It is a favorite of many chemistry teachers for its "wow factor" as a demonstration of oxidation/reduction. The ingredients are cheap and available and the reaction is a controlled, rapid-burning, "explosion" that lights up the classroom. I know of one example of this reaction demonstration gone awry where the chemistry teacher lost several fingers, spattered blood on students in the first rows of seating, and blew a hole the size of a bowling ball in the slate chemistry table at the front of the room. Enough said.

A REMINDER

When an accident or breach of safety occurs in a school, the first person contacted is the building principal. It behooves the principal to have communicated safety requirements, rules, and policies to the faculty and staff. Monitoring of safety issues must continue throughout the school year. Supervision by "wandering about" the building is an excellent strategy.

Protect your job and the safety of your students and staff members by executing all applicable and required Board of Education Policies and Occupational Safety and Health Administration (OSHA) regulations, as well as common sense safety practices.

—⁓—

Chapter 4

OPEN OR CLOSED CAMPUS?

INTRODUCTION

A closed high school campus means that students are not permitted to exit and reenter the campus or building at will during the school day. This restriction would, in its strictest definition, include lunchtime and any other time during the school day that a student is not specifically assigned to be in classes.

Many high schools with a closed campus have "open periods" or time slots where students are not assigned to a classroom with a supervising teacher. Students are expected to occupy their time studying in a library, computer lab, lunchroom, student lounge, or other spaces designated for this purpose. Supervised, mandatory study halls are used in many schools to fill any open periods in a student's day.

An open high school campus allows enrolled students to come and go, on and off campus, any time they are not assigned to a class. Strict attendance in all assigned classes is expected and enforced. Student access to their motor vehicles is usually not restricted.

PROBLEMS ASSOCIATED WITH OPEN CAMPUS

What problems are associated with an open campus? What's all the fuss about anyway? Why not let high school students come and go from campus and the building at will? Aren't high schools preparing their students for college and/or the world of work where these freedoms exist?

Problems associated with a high school open campus include, but are not limited to:

- Traffic accidents during the school day away from campus resulting in damage to property, injuries to persons involved in the accidents, and occasionally deaths.

- Crimes committed by high school students during the school day while off campus such as shop lifting, vandalism, and loitering.

- Traffic violations while off campus for speeding and other common police citations.

- Tardiness to school classes due to poor judgment of time required for returning to campus.

- Missing entire assigned school classes (cutting or unauthorized absence) due to more attractive alternatives off campus.

- Access to alcohol or drugs off campus during the school day and returning to school and classes under the influence.

- Unauthorized departure and/or transport of students forbidden to leave campus by their parents or guardians.

- Visits to students' homes during the school day to engage in unauthorized activities such as alcohol consumption, "partying," and sexual contacts.

- Students who are habitual non-attenders for all or part of the school day may attract marginal or hesitant students to adopt or engage in the same conduct.

- Consistently negative all-school data for student attendance, dropout rate, etc.

- Difficulties in determining who is an enrolled student and who is not. Unwanted or unauthorized visitors mingle with enrolled students.

WHY CLOSE THE CAMPUS?

I am an unabashed advocate for a closed campus at the high school level. I kept data for years after installing a closed campus at the site of my fourth principalship. These data on the modified-closed campus system have demonstrated that commonly kept school statistics reveal positive results. When compared to similar sized high schools with similar student demographics in the same school district, the school with the modified-closed campus consistently had a:

- Higher graduation rate.

- Lower dropout rate.

- Higher percentage of students attending college after graduation.

- Higher average daily attendance.

- Higher percentage of student participation in extracurricular activities.

- Significantly lower "F" rate in freshmen classes. (Fewer "F" grades earned by freshmen.)

PERIODS IN THE SCHOOL DAY AND STUDY HALL

One variable that can be used to approximate a closed campus is the number of periods per day in the schedule with all students assigned to a class every period. Using a five or six period day with all students assigned to a full class schedule, no open periods for students exist and, therefore, only lunch needs to be addressed. Shortened lunch periods also minimize the opportunity for students to depart campus. Working three lunch periods into two standard-length class periods is feasible.

Any arrangement of periods or number of periods can be used in a school if mandatory study halls are added. Free time at lunch still needs to be addressed, but the balance of the school day restricts movement off campus simply by accounting for every student every period. There is no free time other than lunch.

ACCESS TO MOTOR VEHICLES

If the high school campus is arranged or can be modified to strictly control the movement of motor vehicles from the student parking lot, many of the negatives of open campus can be addressed. This will require campus monitors to assure conformance during school hours. Maverick off-campus parking will have to be monitored and controlled. Vehicles parked off campus in the local community, on residential streets, or in parking lots of nearby businesses will frequently draw the ire of those inconvenienced or subject to the trash often dumped by student drivers.

Restricting students to campus may not work well if attractive alternatives to staying on campus are within walking distances that students are willing to risk evading authorities. Fast food restaurants, pizza shops, malls, and convenience stores are powerful magnets to pull students off campus during the school day.

ENFORCEMENT

The success of any attempt at a closed campus will ultimately depend on consistent enforcement. Breakdowns in enforcement will terminate the strategy.

I highly recommend supplying campus security monitors with communication devices and transportation. Golf carts work very well to keep monitors mobile for rapid movement around parking lots and campus grounds. If money is tight for the purchase of a golf cart, solicit parents for a loaner or donation of a cart. A cover can be installed on the cart(s) for wind and winter protection. Indoor parking for the cart at night is highly desirable for battery charging and security.

MODIFIED CLOSED CAMPUS

An alternative to a totally closed high school campus is the modified-closed campus. Under this system, freshmen and sophomores are subject to the rules and regulations of the closed campus while juniors and seniors have open campus privileges if they qualify for an "off-campus pass." It is also desirable under the modified-closed campus plan to place all ninth and tenth graders with open periods in a supervised study hall setting. There is an unintended positive consequence of requiring mandatory study halls. High percentages of ninth and tenth graders will enroll in the maximum number of classes to avoid having open periods requiring them to be assigned to study halls.

PARENT CONTROLS

There is an important component to a modified closed campus that must not be overlooked. It is essential to require parents to provide written permission for their eligible student to have the privilege to participate in the modified open-campus program. Eligible students with written parent permission are issued a picture ID "off-campus pass" that must be displayed upon request by staff members. Parents may revoke their permission for this pass at any time during the school year.

The wisdom of this requirement rests on giving parents control over their student. If off-campus problems occur, the parent is a partner with the school. Either the parent or the school can revoke off-campus privileges. The parent can withdraw permission for any reason, and the school can revoke the pass for cause. Having one more penalty for discipline is helpful for maintaining good order among upper classmen. The revocation penalty can be short or long term depending on the offense.

TRANSITIONING TO A CLOSED CAMPUS

Moving from an open to a closed campus can be a Herculean task not to be undertaken without an approved long-term plan. Students and many of their parents will not go willingly down the road from open to closed. Established high school populations view open campus as a right, not a privilege. Most students and many parents could care less about the purported benefits of a closed campus.

With board of education approval and plan in hand, the slowest and highest probability for success would follow a one-grade-per-year phase in. Start with the incoming freshmen class. Add a class a year as each grade moves up. You could stop after two years if you prefer the modified-closed campus discussed above.

Going cold turkey by attempting to implement a fully closed campus involving all four grades in one year could be a backbreaker and end in a reversal to a fully open campus. I am familiar with one large comprehensive high school that took eight years to move from totally open to a totally closed campus.

There is one scenario that might demand quicker movement to a closed campus. Should a tragic accident, perhaps a death, occur in the community during the school day involving high school students, the superintendent or board of education could be subjected to enormous pressure from parents and the community to mandate a closed-campus arrangement. This is especially true if the accident is perceived by the public to have been preventable under a closed-campus system.

—∿—

Chapter 5

EXTRACURRICULAR ACTIVITIES

INTRODUCTION

Extracurricular activities, sometimes called co-curricular activities, are one of the keys to a highly successful and productive school. I define highly successful and productive when referring to a school that:

- Meets the traditional expectations of high academic achievement.

- Exhibits a positive school climate for all students.

- Posts graduation rates above 98%.

- Demonstrates exceptional preparation for life after graduation.

- Graduates students that are highly satisfied with their school experience.

One of the needs of American high school teenagers is a genuine connection to their school. I believe that link is more firmly cemented when a very high percentage of students are engaged in extracurricular activities.

The quality of the educational experience for students is vastly different between a school averaging 20% of their students participating in one or more after-school activities when compared to another school averaging 80% participation. Maintaining data on this area at your school is very important to monitor current status and progress over time.

It is essential to understand that after-school activities include not only traditional sports, music, and drama, but also an incredibly rich variety of clubs and organizations that appeal to groups of students with diverse interests and talents. Capturing the time and efforts of these students are what will drive a school closer to an 80% after-school participation rate.

The last high school I supervised had 1500 students that averaged 83% after-school participation by students in grades 9-12. The percentage figure means that 1245 of the school's 1500 students participated in at least one of the after-school activities during the school year. Many students participated in more than one after-school activity, but they were only counted once.

PARTICIPATION NUMBERS IN SPORTS

I have observed two varieties of sports coaches over the years that produce different results regarding participation rates. The first stereotype seeks, attracts, and holds very high numbers of student participants in his/her sport. There seems to be room for every student interested and willing to participate. Cutting or dropping a student from the team for other than safety or health reasons is unheard of and does not happen. This stereotype is more prevalent in sports like swimming, track and field, cross country, and wrestling. Sometimes these sports are referred to as individual sports (and contrasted with team sports) since individuals can earn honors with or without the entire team doing the same.

Team sport coaches seeking and achieving high numbers of participants do so by adding as many levels of competition as possible to encourage retention and development. They eschew the cutting or dropping of students perceived to have poor skill levels. Again, team coaches also attend to individuals whose health or safety might be compromised by participation.

The second stereotype of a sports coach is one who pays particular attention and interest in the student participants achieving at the highest level of the sport. Coaching time and effort are focused on the high achievers to the detriment of recruiting, growing, and developing novices. Coaching satisfaction seems to come from the achievements of the more elite participants. Examples would include individual state champions, nationally ranked teams or individuals, or those earning college scholarships to play at the next level.

While I don't believe that these two stereotypic coaches are mutually exclusive, a simple head count of participants is an indication of the tendency. If you lean towards my bias of high levels of student participation in all after-school activities, you will look a little deeper into the coaching history of a candidate before making a job offer. For candidates with no history, ask about their philosophy. I believe at the high school level that numbers of participants really do count. It is important for coaches to actively, perhaps aggressively, recruit, encourage, and develop the students.

On a related note, it is very important to establish parameters for what I call "coach competition" for highly talented participants within the schoolhouse. Negative school climate will emanate from Draconian coaches seeking to corner and hold the market on athletes. Not "allowing" athletes to participate on other high school sports teams so they will engage in elaborate "off season" practices and conditioning is unacceptable. This behavior is an example of rash, ill-advised conduct that will set the tone for the entire sports program and, perhaps, the entire school. If successful, these coaches will create a polarized school that is what I call a one-sport or one-activity high school. Indicators of a problem are characterized by coaches who:

- Fail to be supportive of all sports in the school.

- Rank their activity as more important than any other.

- Discourage or restrict "their athletes" from participation on other teams.

- Apply pressure on students to follow their philosophy.

- Contact parents to advance their off-season agenda.

- Discourage or prohibit "their" athletes from skiing or other activities that might cause injury.

A ONE TEAM OR ONE ACTIVITY HIGH SCHOOL

Before I pick on sports as my example of the detrimental effects of putting all your time, attention, efforts, and money on one, dominate after-school activity to the exclusion of others, let me highlight another potential attention grabber. In many high schools, it is not a sports team, but a band or other program, that defines the school, again, pretty much to the exclusion of other activities.

This high school is often identified by and known in the community as the "band school." If a student is into music, performance orientated, or wanting to play (or continue to play after middle school) a musical instrument in high school, then they are "encouraged" to attend high school "X" (especially in a multi-high district). Extremely high parent participation with truly high hands-on involvement is a cornerstone of this single-activity program. Independent-parent fund raising takes on gargantuan proportions that are directly related to the continued annual success of the program. The financial support of other after-school activity programs in the school usually pale by comparison.

Let's be clear, the key to what's being said here is that the principal should create and provide the leadership to promote all after-school activity programming. The reason should be evident. High school students need as many choices, options, and opportunities as possible. Participation in the art club, school yearbook, or technology club is as important and critical to the student involved, as is the position of football quarterback, president of student government, or band drum major. All of these activities, opportunities, and positions connect students to the school, adult supervision and guidance, and validation outside the home.

Don't be a one-team or one-activity high school. One program cannot "win" at the expense of another. Keep the wonderful, high functioning teams and activities that you have and get others activated and inspired to do the same. Do not fall victim to the illogical and fallacious argument that if you push other teams or activities up, others must or will come down. This is a win/lose mentality. Adopt a win/win philosophy. Leadership will have to work hard and long to ameliorate negative thinking and negative actions and get everyone moving in the same positive direction.

THE "CROSS COUNTRY AND ORCHESTRA" YARDSTICK

If you are looking for your first high school principalship or looking to change locations for another principalship, I have one idea for you to consider when researching new schools. Based on the biases I have expressed and outlined above, look closely at a potential new school to see if they have a cross-country team and an orchestra. In addition, if the school has both activities, note the number of program participants and the gender balance of each.

Based strictly on personal, observational data, I have noted that high schools with these two programs with large numbers of participants in each and close gender parity in each approximate an ideal setting for all involved in the enterprise. To say that another way, these two programs with high participation and gender balance are indicators of the overall condition of the rest of the school.

Here are some thoughts or rationale for this conclusion. If a student is able to walk down the main hallway during school with his/her violin case clearly visible without hassle, wisecracks, or irritation from fellow students, you can be assured that the school has:

- A positive school climate.

- Tolerance and acceptance of diversity.

- A well-established code of conduct among students that is mutually supporting of all enrolled in the school.

If the orchestra student being described is male, you can also remove macho and bravado as negative behaviors likely to be encountered on the way to the music room.

Cross-country running, like playing a musical instrument, requires:

- Personal discipline and accountability.

- Hours of practice.

- Year around practice.

- Pain at times.

- Focus.

- Thinking.

- Good time management.

- Sustained motivation.

Off-the-track distance running is one of the least glamorous high school sports imaginable. Training to plod over three miles, often in very cold and wet weather, is highly demanding. Students willing to engage in cross-country running in large numbers with gender balance indicate a group with moxie that I think bolsters the entire school.

Behind every orchestra player and cross-country runner stands parents who encourage, support, and nurture these pursuits. These same parents contribute greatly to the backbone of school programming and support for the entire school.

There are other high school programs that could be equally described here to provide substance to my rationale, but orchestra and cross-country consistently have led my list of indicators of a quality school with numerous opportunities for greatness.

TRANSPORTING STUDENTS TO AND FROM ACTIVITIES IN PRIVATE VEHICLES

An often-neglected sector of daily school life is school employees transporting enrolled students in private vehicles on official school activities. Examples of official school activities include:

- Approved school field trips.

- Transportation to/from sports practice locations, contests, or other competitions.

- Transportation to/from school-approved club or other after-school or organization activities.

- Transporting students to purchase school supplies, food, or equipment.

My first advice to principals is to be sure to check on and enforce board of education policies regarding this topic for faculty/ staff, parents, and students. I am aware of many high schools that regularly violate board policy because the rules seem too restrictive and just plain inconvenient. After all, what could go wrong?

Let's consider a traffic accident involving a student driving fellow students to athletic practices. No matter how minor, it can and has resulted in litigation beyond belief. A traffic accident resulting in bodily injury to students or the death of a student will paralyze a school for an indefinite period of time. Administrators may be moved, replaced, or terminated.

After an accident, the board of education, superintendent, and building principal are frequently co-defendants in one or more lawsuits for failure to enforce their own written policy prohibiting students or school employees from transporting students in their private vehicles to and from school activities.

Another very difficult scenario results when school employees thinking that they are somehow "covered" under vehicle collision and liability insurance carried by the board of education transports students and finds out that they are, in fact, in violation of board policy with no coverage or legal protection.

A reality that principals must face in this day and age is that a sexual predator who unbeknownst to the principal has worked his/her way into the schoolhouse, perhaps as a volunteer. Now this person has an excellent opportunity to exercise his/her negative intentions by offering to drive a student home after a sports contest, practice, or other after-hours school activity. While this might be a very difficult sequence of events to predict and prevent, the principal can add one more barrier for the perpetrator to overcome. This is done by issuing clear and frequent verbal warnings and written copies of the board policy on the transportation of students in private vehicles.

I should also point out that with proper notice to the faculty and staff of board policy the principal is also providing a modicum of protection to naïve and well-intentioned employees. For example, they may find themselves alone in their motor vehicle with a

EXTRACURRICULAR ACTIVITIES

hysterical student who later makes false claims of inappropriate employee conduct and contact. Sorry to sound maudlin and like a curmudgeon but unfortunately these things happen. Protect, or at least warn, school personnel at every opportunity.

—◊◊—

47

Chapter 6

COACHES, SPONSORS & SCHOOL CLIMATE

INTRODUCTION

I want to deviate a bit from conventional conversation about the high school principalship and bring up what I consider an often-overlooked element that makes and sometimes breaks positive school climate. School climate is literally what students "feel" about their school environment when they interact with their school. Do they feel upbeat, positive, safe, relaxed, welcomed, reassured, be-friended, cared for, included, happy, and supported? Or do they feel isolated, generally negative, uncertain, tense, cliquishness, and discouraged?

Are interactions among students warm, respectful, caring, friendly, helpful, across grade levels, civil, and generally calm? Or are student interactions curt, rude and brief, ignored, laced with profanities, subject to bravado, scary at times, disrespect-ful, and often characterized by seemingly random out-of-control physical slaps and smacks? Are the interactions between students and teachers more like the positive or negative set of descrip-tors? Observing the type of interactions in the school can help the principal gage the school's climate to determine if it needs improvement.

The Importance of Coaches, Coaching Assistants, and Sponsors

I have made the case in other chapters that ultra high percentages of student participation in extracurricular or co-curricular school activities are an essential component of a high-functioning, high-achieving school. Connecting students to their school through this mechanism also generates high levels of satisfaction with the high school experience among students and their parents and leads to positive school climate. I now need to insert a qualifier that influences the student experience either positively or negatively.

Teenagers will frequently follow and adopt the behaviors and language of school personnel serving as their mentors. Teenagers in our culture often struggle when left on their own without an adult role model. They generally lack the experience and skills necessary to separate acts of civility and sweetness in one setting with grossness and rude conduct in the next setting.

Many student athletes cannot modulate these behaviors and language that sometimes crossover between settings at inopportune times and places during the school day. The net effect of negative crossover behaviors contributes to an overall negative school climate. The effect is amplified on the balance of the student population because these same student athletes often serve as models for their fellow students, particularly underclassmen.

Below is one example of a coach in a particular sport. I need to emphasize that this sequence of events can be applied to any coach and activity sponsor in the school. For example, the after-school drama and theatre coach will also contribute to the positive or negative school climate being described.

Football Scenario

I'm going to start with, or some might think, "pick on," the head varsity football coach for my example. I contend that the members of the football team positively or negatively influence the school climate in the American public high school. Since football begins in the fall and extends into the semester for several months, I also contend that whatever climate is set in the fall continues for the balance of the school year. I think the good news is that the principal has influence and control over the state of affairs I am arguing.

The following is a negative scenario from coaching conduct to school climate. I maintain that a coach, who uses, allows, encourages, or models profanity, gives de facto permission to the players to duplicate those behaviors or language. This would also include physical taunting, verbal abuse, and intimidation in interactions with other coaches and as well as with players. Many times the players also assume the roles of stereotypic alpha males that serve to exaggerate even more the undesirable, unnecessary, and uncivil conduct and language. Those behaviors can translate directly into daily interactions with fellow students and teachers during the regular school day.

The positive scenario from coaching conduct to school climate is the antithesis of the events described above. When a coach expresses, models, and enforces ironclad rules *against* profanity, aggressive behaviors off the field, bravado, uncivil conduct, rude talk, inflated attitude, and privilege, the positive effect on school climate is staggeringly huge. I have observed and experienced these two extreme examples in my own career. The positive scenario was incredibly uplifting for the entire school.

HIRING, MONITORING, AND EVALUATING COACHES AND SPONSORS

A major opportunity a principal has to affect a positive school climate is to be involved in the hiring process. Expectations and parameters for conduct must be set before the contracts are offered. Commitments for behaviors and language must be confirmed and resumes must be checked thoroughly prior to any extra-duty contracts being signed. It is absolutely necessary to get on the phone or visit previous work locations.

Once on the job, monitoring of behaviors and language usage must occur. Use written warnings and personal meetings to curtail violations of the original agreements and expectations at the time of hiring. Written evaluations specifically targeted at performance while coaching should be separate from classroom performance evaluations. Repeated violations of stated expectations must result in termination. If the principal is serious about the importance and non-negotiable nature of appropriate coaching behaviors and language, they must follow through with termination after documentation of unfulfilled commitments on the part of the coach. This must be done regardless of the win/loss record or popularity of the coach.

As a precursor to assuring the positive behaviors and language of coaches, the principal must be confident that the assistant principal charged with athletic director duties and responsibilities is on the same page as the principal regarding these interests. Any breakdown between principal and assistant principal will torpedo the focus.

I feel the need to emphasize that skilled coaches with leadership expertise do exist; they can and will interact with high school students without resorting to profanity, physical taunting, verbal abuse, and intimidation as essential tools of coaching. They can be found, but it may take time, effort, and patience. The overall potential impact on the entire school is worth the energy expended.

Extra Scrutiny is Justified

Given the realities of current media reports regarding felony offenses by school personnel against students, it is just good judgment for the principal or his designees to spend extra time filtering applicants for extracurricular activities. Hopefully the district has procedures in place for this task. Being sure all adults exposed to students are scrutinized appropriately is the responsibility of the principal.

Background checks are especially important for part-time employees and volunteers who work during school hours and after the regular school day. Many of these folks move under the radar of traditional screening efforts. The reality is that individuals with evil intentions and uncontrolled urges gravitate to youth organizations and often view our students as prey. This distressing fact of life mandates that principals develop a systematic observation of personnel attached to the school in classrooms, on playing fields, locker rooms, and around practice spaces, before and after regular school hours.

When it comes to protecting our students, no one is above reproach. Be vigilant and proactive.

In/Out-of-School Coaches and Sponsors

It has become increasingly difficult to locate and retain quality coaches and sponsors who also hold a classroom teaching position in the building. Finding a job opening on the faculty that matches a coaching vacancy is problematic. In addition, most union agreements separate teaching contracts from extra-duty contracts. This means that coaches or sponsors who are terminated from their extra-duty contracts very often retain their teaching positions.

Dependence on coaches and sponsors from the community who are not otherwise affiliated with the school or district presents challenges.

- Communications with the out-of-school coach or sponsor are demanding.

- Out-of-school coach/sponsor employees have little or no idea what the students arriving at practice have experienced during the regular school day.

- Administrator contact with these employees is minimal making leadership and on-the-job expectations complicated.

- Communicating positive and negative school climate issues to out-of-school employees can be tough.

- Winning can become a narrow and singular focus for out-of-school employees.

- Recruiting and retaining students for the team or club will be more difficult.

- Out-of-school employees contact with students during the school day is lost.

- Monitoring player conduct and progress during the school day is difficult. Coach/sponsor contact with classroom teachers can be essential for collaborative and positive mentoring of struggling individuals.

- Out-of-school coaches/sponsors may not understand and enforce school rules resulting in frustration for all concerned.

- Out-of-school employees have a history of being on the staff for the short term. The potential advantages of stabilizing a program remain problematic.

Solutions for these issues should be a high priority for the principal and assistant principals. Personal and timely contact with out-of-school employees to review the problems listed above will go a long way towards ameliorating potential negative effects on students, parents, and the school.

—◊—

Chapter 7

HAZING

INTRODUCTION

Hazing is defined as students performing humiliating and some-times dangerous initiation rituals. The problem of students hazing students has been in our high schools for more years than the acts deserve. Why hazing survives is imbedded in the developmental needs of teenagers in our culture and our old nemesis, "tradition." "Someone did it to me, so I have the right to do it to the next guy." Sound familiar? Dominating someone with lesser social skills, lower on the teenage pecking order, or with inferior physical attributes may give the perpetrator(s) a psychological boost that blocks out common sense and empathy. However, the etiology of hazing remains an enigma.

Eliminating hazing is a huge step towards a positive school climate where all students have the right to feel safe, secure, and valued in their school. All students must be welcome at their school. There cannot be second-class students who have to undergo rights of passage to be accepted in sports, clubs, and all other extracurricular activities. School personnel cannot foster a climate that encourages and allows enrolled students a free range of opportunities to haze new students.

Faculty, Staff, and Students

For schools experiencing hazing activities and events, I would recommend that the principal contemplate an assault on and elimination of hazing with a written outline of an implementation plan. It is highly likely that resistance to actions to halt hazing will be encountered. The written plan should deal with both specific acts of hazing and hazing in general. An implementation timetable will keep the principal focused in the midst of objections, anger, subversion, and possible sabotage.

The first part of the implementation plan should be addressed to the faculty followed shortly thereafter by an address to non-certificated staff. The timetable might begin with notice to these two groups in the spring before departing for the summer. Inservice days before students arrive in the fall might also be a choice. The principal must judge how much time is needed to receive, understand, process, and accept the anti-hazing edict by staff.

The next group to receive the new order of conduct regarding hazing is the student body. This can be accomplished in an all-school assembly led by the principal or in a homeroom environment led by individual faculty members. Input from the faculty regarding the preferred interface with the students is valuable and recommended.

Coaches and Club Sponsors

In several of the schools I served, I initially introduced the anti-hazing plan by special meetings with our coaches and club sponsors. Much to my surprise and naïveté, I discovered many of our sport coaches, club sponsors, music and theatre teachers, and other extracurricular sponsors, both male and female, encouraged, sponsored, conducted, and supervised hazing activities. Most of these adults referred to these sanctioned hazing activities as "initiations."

Let me be as clear as I can be, initiations are hazing. They have no place in a public high school. They cannot be justified under any form of argument. They are not fun, funny, cute, innocent, harmless, or necessary. They neither build team nor teamwork. Turning teenagers loose to devise humiliating and sometimes dangerous initiation rituals is just bizarre and escapes definition. Hazing activities can and do escalate out of control in an instant. People get hurt. People are traumatized.

One of the biggest obstacles to overcome when shutting down these hazing activities is tradition. The only major advice I can give is to state the new order of things at your school, put your foot down, and publicize your unalterable position verbally and in writing. Then you must monitor and enforce the "no hazing" rule as needed with students, parents, and staff. A change of this magnitude in most high schools and most communities will take time and effort.

If the superintendent and board of education fail to support you, you may not last the school year. So, do your homework before you start. If you articulate the down side of school initiation activities, the unnecessary harm experienced by many individuals undergoing these traditions, and seek support from what I believe are the silent majority against initiations and hazing, you can establish a pathway to eliminate it from your school.

THE SCHOOL COMMUNITY

On or about the same time you launch your anti-hazing plan within your school, you must also pay attention to your community and parents. Many parents will oppose your anti-hazing efforts because they have memories of their own hazing traditions. They view initiations as part of high school life with few negatives. You may have to seek other parents who were scared to death to move from

8th to 9th grade at their local high school. You should consider a multipronged approach.

- Send a direct mailing to all school parents explaining the problems surrounding hazing at the school, your solutions, and behavior expectations under the (new) rules being implemented and enforced including penalties for violations.

- Hold an evening meeting at the school for all interested parents so that you can restate the problems, goals, objectives, and expectations to halt hazing at the school. One spinoff from a meeting like this is clear feedback from a key constituency, your parents. A big turnout loaded with negative criticism of the new attack on hazing will tell you that you're in for a longer overhaul than anticipated. A sparse turnout with mostly positive supporters will provide impetus to move forward with all due haste.

- Be sure to inform your supervisors about your anti-hazing efforts before you start and update them as needed once the program is underway. It's highly likely that they will receive contacts of inquiry such as, "Can he (you) really do this?" If your supervisors are not informed, onboard, and in support of your efforts, you're doomed before you start.

HAZING PAR EXCELLENCE

Perhaps a personal experience will help make the point that hazing has no place in a public school. In my very first high school principalship, I was hired in a semi-rural community with about 500 students in grades 9-12. The Superintendent and Board of Education made it clear that they expected me bring order and discipline to their "out of control" high school.

In the very first days of the school year in the fall, I was informed of a hazing activity in progress during lunchtime. Several freshmen boys were taken against their will, put in the back of a pickup truck, transported one mile on a country road to the community cemetery, striped of their clothing, and left nude to make their way back to town.

As I investigated the event and began to discipline the perpetrators, I was baffled at the parental responses. Parent after parent verbally pummeled me "explaining" that not only was this a time-honored tradition in the community but also that it had persevered for years and generations. In short, I had no business, much less authority, to take an anti-hazing posture.

So, on the one hand, I had several devastated freshmen boys with injuries sustained while being restrained in the back of the pickup on the way to the cemetery, and on the other side, parents of the guilty perpetrators telling me to back off and "lighten up." No harm, no foul. (As an aside, the local police wanted nothing to do with the situation. I was on my own. This was a "school problem.")

After conferencing with the superintendent and receiving his re-confirmation of the directive to restore order to the school, I moved with all due haste to set the new direction for the school that included no hazing and no initiations. Things settled down for a few weeks until a similar incident occurred.

A group of girls decided to duplicate the boys trip to the cemetery by taking a freshman girl against her will to the site, removing all her clothes, and leaving her to make her way back to town. The community was horrified! Interestingly, the outpouring of distress and disgust did not focus on the activity or act of hazing, but rather that it was a female who was the victim. Apparently a female had never been targeted in the past.

As a rookie-building principal, I was presented with a community value held by many parents that supported dangerous, violent, and frightening hazing activities against young males but definitely not females. This presented one of several interesting dilemmas for my future at this school.

Unfortunately, I have many, many more examples and experiences involving hazing spanning thirty years that could fill a small book by themselves. However, I'll end the true story outlined above by saying that it took many years to alter community perceptions and establish a safe, productive school before I moved on to new challenges in my second principalship.

—⚍—

Chapter 8

STUDENT LOCKERS

INTRODUCTION

The assignment, arrangement, and distribution of students to school-owned lockers are a significant control point for achieving and maintaining reasonable building decorum and student safety. This includes all types of student lockers: hall, gym, art, photography, and music.

I have never really understood why so many principals have missed the importance of locker assignments. Tradition, student status, and privilege are the only common reasons I have heard over the thirty years I worked in and visited America's high schools.

If you are moving to a principalship with a mandate to reduce harassment, eliminate bullying, build positive school climate, and make the common hallways lined with student lockers less scary and intimidating, then please take this chapter seriously.

LOCATION OF HALL LOCKERS (LOCKER BANKS)

Senior Hall

I was hired at two separate high schools over the years that maintained a tradition of placing most, if not all, seniors in hall lockers stretching down two sides of a common hallway. What I observed upon students entering the first days of school was unexpected and unacceptable. Only seniors were "allowed" to use what the student body referred to as "the senior hallway." Many uninformed freshmen were introduced to the tradition by harsh means that produced laughter and delight among fellow seniors. Within days, grades nine through eleven learned or knew to avoid travel down "senior hall." As I sought clarity from students and faculty members, it became apparent that this "tradition," some called it a "privilege," had been sanctioned for many years. Upon reflection, my personal thoughts ranged from anger to disbelief. I ended senior hall and suffered the wrath of the seniors for the balance of the school year.

Seniors were distraught that this school-sanctioned privilege to harass and haze their fellow undergrads was summarily taken from them. Even some juniors and a few of their parents complained mightily that eliminating senior hall was going to ruin their senior year because "...they were harassed as undergrads and looked forward to passing it on." It was simply going to be their earned right and their time to intimidate and harass the newbie's. After a year or two, the fury passed and we moved on.

Freshmen Hall

In similar fashion, I visited several high schools over the years that placed all hall locker assignments for freshmen in the same hallway. What I observed in one school was the perfect storm for targeting ninth graders. From a floor above the exposed freshmen locker area, fellow students could and did literally heave whatever they had in their hands down upon the lowly plebes. The area was trashed throughout the day of my visit. The general behavior of the students milling about the freshmen locker area was very middle schoolish and not conducive to positive school climate.

My advice is not to create a freshmen hall locker area. I really do not see any benefits to the students or the school. In fact, granting "privileged" status to any group within the school will undermine a healthy and robust school climate.

NOTICE TO PARENTS AND STUDENTS

The very first step in taking control of all school-owned student lockers is to annually publish a notice to parents and students in all appropriate publications citing the Board of Education Policy regarding the topic. This is usually located in the Board Policy Manual under "searches." It is essential for principals to regularly publish in appropriate school documents, such as the student handbook, that all lockers, desks, and storage spaces provided for student use at the school and on school premises are school property.

As such, these items and locations remain at all times under the control of the school. It is very important to state clearly that school authorities retain the right to open or enter lockers, desks, and storage spaces and inspect the contents for any reason at any time without notice or student consent. The policy should also state that only locks provided or approved by school authorities may be used on school property and that unapproved locks will be removed and destroyed.

The stage is now set to maintain order and discipline in the school and to protect the safety and welfare of students and school personnel. Judicial use of this authority by school personnel is the responsibility of the principal.

ASSIGNMENT TO HALL LOCKERS

A principal's first option in issuing hall lockers to students is to provide no choices. Students arrive at registration and are handed a hall locker number and lock combination. If two or more students at your school must share a hall locker, the same procedure is followed. The school simply uses some system, random or otherwise, to make the assignments.

Another option available is to allow limited student choices for hall lockers. A principal can establish necessary and desirable limits while allowing student choices. For example, in a four-grade high school, every fourth student hall locker could be designated for a ninth grader, tenth grader, etc. This approach maximizes grade mixing. As students register, they would be allowed to select a hall locker from a floor location map with hall lockers designated for their grade level only.

If this is too limiting, two hall lockers in a row could be designated for each grade level. So, in eight hall lockers, the first two would be for grade nine, the second two for grade ten, etc., with the sequence repeating throughout the school.

One option I found especially effective in getting rapid results to help stabilize a negative climate high school was assigning students to hall lockers by the alphabet. While being random in nature and nondiscriminatory, an interesting secondary benefit emerged. Using the alphabet placed brothers and sisters in adjacent hall lockers. Most were in different grades. Hanging around hall lockers and undesirable behaviors around hall lockers diminished substantially. Apparently periodic, close, unsupervised proximity to siblings had a chilling effect on negative behaviors.

STUDENTS CHANGING LOCKER ASSIGNMENTS

Students who are unhappy with their hall locker assignment will engage in negative behaviors to correct their predicament. In the worst-case scenario, a student will intimidate another student to obtain a hall locker in a more favorable location in the school. The intimidation could be physical harm or the threat of physical harm. Bribing, trading, or purchasing a change of locker location are also possible negatives.

The school secretary or hall monitor in charge of student hall locker assignments is a key person to control students changing hall locker assignments. Hall locker combination lock numbers should only be reissued to the student who was initially issued the lock and locker. Any number of lame excuses will be given by students attempting to access and enter a hall locker not assigned to them.

Emergency Access to Student Lockers

It is essential that all student lockers (hall, gym, art, photography, music, etc.) be secured with school-provided or preapproved locking devices. It should be placed in writing (student handbook) that unapproved locks or impediments would be removed and destroyed without prior notice and without reimbursement for the loss.

Two primary locking devices fit the requirements for rapid school access: individual combination padlocks that have a master key keyway at the rear of the device and built-in combination locks that have a master key keyway in the center front of the lock. Manufacturers of the second type also offer five or more alternate combinations in the same lock allowing combination changes at the end of each school year in preparation for the next school year.

The primary purpose for the establishment and maintenance of this level of security is to expedite locker searches in safety and emergency situations. The school must have the following immediately available in the administrative area of the school:

- One or two very large and powerful bolt cutters.

- At least ten sets of locker master keys.

- Floor by floor maps of student locker locations and numbers.

Building administrators and other appropriate school personnel must be aware of and comfortable with these items for deployment as necessary.

In a worst-case scenario, a credible bomb threat, the sets of student locker master keys would be distributed to school personnel or first responders to rapidly open student lockers as determined by the building or district emergency response plan. Occasional maverick or unauthorized locking devices would be quickly removed using the husky bolt cutters. In the absence of school-provided locks, cutting off literally hundreds, perhaps well over a thousand, hall-locker locks would be unnecessarily prohibitive. Time delays could be problematic.

On occasion, school authorities might initiate or capitulate to outside pressure (police or parent groups, for example) for a building-wide student-locker search for banned items such as drugs, weapons, alcohol, stolen goods, etc. Most often these searches would be conducted when students were not present such as on weekends or well after regular school hours. Maintaining the three items listed above in the administrative area will expedite and reasonably organize a rapid and focused search of the school.

—⁓—

Chapter 9

RELIGION IN THE SCHOOL

INTRODUCTION

One of the topics that frequently surfaces in a public high school is religion. Hopefully, your board of education has clear, written rules and regulations in policy that guide and direct your words and deeds when issues surrounding religion and religion in the school emerge. This subject has the potential to challenge your leadership skills to the maximum. I recommend that you maintain several copies of your board of education policies on religion in your office. One of your responsibilities is to help educate your constituent groups on this important topic.

During my last twenty years as a building principal, I worked for a school district that is often recognized as having one of the best Board of Education Policies on "teaching about religion and religion in the schools." The language is so succinct that it would be foolhardy for me to attempt my own description of the topic or paraphrase their policy. Therefore, I will encourage you to view the policy in its entirety by searching Google online at:

- Boulder Valley School District, Boulder, Colorado.

- Look for Boulder Valley School District (BVSD) Board of Education.

- Look for the heading "related board links," and click on "BVSD Policies and Regulations."

- In the portion of the screen titled "search this site," enter policy code IGAC-R.

- You may now read or print all five pages of this valuable policy.

I encourage you to compare the BVSD policy on religion in the schools with similar board of education policies in your school district.

Topics Covered

To whet your interest and encourage you to view this policy, I will list the subheadings of the sections under policy code IGAC-R:

- A. Neutrality.

- B. Teaching About Religion and School Programs.

- C. Student Expression of Religious Belief.

- D. School Assemblies, Sponsoring Religious Groups, and Use of Religious Facilities for Special Programs.

- E. School Visitors.

- F. Use of School Facilities by Nonstudent Religious Groups or Other Organizations.

- G. Baccalaureate Services, Invocations, and Benedictions.

- H. Staff Religious Groups.

FIRST JOB, CHANGING JOBS, CHANGING DISTRICTS

The subject of religion in the schools may find you polarized at one end of the spectrum or the other and unable or unwilling to assume and advocate the neutral stance required by law while on the job as principal of a public school. In this situation, it would be wise and prudent for you to research these issues prior to your first job as a principal, prior to changing jobs to a principalship, or prior to changing districts in the same job as a principal.

A public school by definition welcomes and serves all students in its attendance area. Diversity within the population to be served is almost a universal standard. Students with an atheist up bringing may be seated in your classrooms next to students from homes where strict adherence to religious doctrine is sacrosanct. Assuming and exuding the position of neutrality regarding religion while on the job at school is the only defensible posture for a public school principal. Conveying neutrality regarding religion to the staff and faculty is another leadership challenge and requirement.

You can and should maintain your internal feelings and beliefs on these subjects, but on the job, as principal of a public school, you will need to assume the neutral position as outlined in the BVSD policies cited and, hopefully, the board of education policies of your school district. If you cannot meet the expectations of the policies of the new job or new district you are investigating, stay where you are at present or seek an alternative.

An alternative for a principal candidate struggling with the issues of neutrality on the job regarding religion would be serious consideration of a private school or religion-based school.

—⚏—

Chapter 10

PERSONNEL EVALUATIONS

INTRODUCTION

In most high school settings, the building principal is responsible for performance evaluations for all personnel under his/her jurisdiction. The size of the institution can make it impossible for one person, no matter how competent, to complete all staff evaluations. Delegation is required if the task is to be completed on time and in good order.

The principal is usually required to countersign and date all written evaluations below the signatures of the evaluatee and primary evaluator. This essentially signifies and certifies that the principal has read the document and agrees with and endorses the contents and conclusions. The principal may delegate authority for these tasks but retains responsibility and accountability.

DELEGATION OF AUTHORITY

My first recommendation is to prepare or have your head secretary prepare lists of all staff members in the zone for evaluation in the current school year. District policies and union agreements usually dictate the individuals that must undergo this examination during any given school year. It is essential that no one who is eligible be exempt from these lists.

Questions of marginality must be settled early in the school year. Personnel added after the start of the school year must be adjudicated for possible inclusion on the lists. Personnel transferring from another school in the district often require special scrutiny to determine their status for evaluation in your building for the current school year.

Once you are comfortable that the list or lists are current and accurate, sit down with your assistant principal(s) and any others who might be in the position of primary evaluator. Others might include the building head secretary, the head custodian, security chief, head of special education in the building, or head building counselor to name a few possibilities. Union agreements may dictate that certificated personnel may only be evaluated by building administrators, so the initial meeting with everyone involved in the evaluation process should deal first with classified personnel.

CLASSIFIED PERSONNEL

Classified personnel that may be up for evaluation during the current school year include:

- Paraprofessionals.

- Secretaries.

- Custodians.

- Bus drivers.

- Kitchen personnel.

- Security monitors.

- Non-certified sports head coaches and assistant coaches.

- Library aides.

- Technology specialists or aides.

- School nurse.

Some of these employees get evaluated every school year, and some in alternate years. Decide who in the meeting of potential evaluators is accepting responsibility for which individuals on the list(s). Verbally review expectations for the task, set the tone for the pending interactions, and hand out written guidelines. Distribute written timelines with deadlines that agree with union and district documents. Review and handout all evaluation documents to be used, signed, and subsequently submitted to the building principal in a timely manner. Provide "safety valves" for the evaluators if the process with an evaluatee unexpectedly deteriorates. (Safety valves were discussed in Chapter One.)

CERTIFICATED PERSONNEL

Classified evaluators may be dismissed from the meeting or a second meeting should be planned with only the principal and assistant principal(s) to discuss and review certificated personnel evaluations.

I believe in an equitable distribution among assistant principals of the number of certified evaluations to be performed. An opportunity for debate on the wisdom or practicality of such distribution should be provided with an open mind and attentive ear to the arguments. Assistant principals may give and take evaluatees based on a number of concerns. For example, an AP may have completed an evaluation on a particular classroom teacher during the last school year. This is a good reason for another AP to place that person on his/her personal list assignment for the current school year. Two evaluations on the same teacher by two different AP's are preferable to two from the same AP two or three years in a row.

Another reason for selecting a particular evaluatee can be based on the assistant principal's curricular background. Instructional prowess and content knowledge in the classroom might be divergent rather than convergent. To say that another way, a teacher might display exceptional instructional skills but with weak or seriously lacking content knowledge. Following the designated curriculum may also be an issue more likely detected by an administrator with an academic background in the content area.

My advice and preference for selecting certified personnel to evaluate for the school year would favor the principal taking as many first, second, and/or third year teachers as possible. The assistant principals should divvy up the balance of what used to be called tenured teachers, those with three or more years of contract experience in the building/district. My rationale for this distribution is based on the high stakes decisions that must be made regarding retention or non-retention of teachers new to the building/district.

Retention can also be defined as making a decision to offer a teacher or other certified personnel a contract for the following school year. So, in effect, the principal does not recommend firing a teacher, but rather fails to offer that teacher a contract for the next school year. Conformance with the union or meet-and-confer rules established by the board of education is absolutely necessary. Deadlines in the agreements for official notification of non-renewal must be met.

Many school administrators agree that decisions regarding retention or non-retention of certified personnel are the most important recommendations made in the course of a school year. The quality of the instructional staff and fulfillment of the commitment to have a highly qualified and productive teacher in every classroom every school day starts with these decisions. Since the principal will almost certainly have to visit the classrooms of identified marginal teachers, it is prudent and efficient to have the assignment in the first place.

CLASSROOM VISITS

The question frequently arises from assistant principals regarding the number of classroom visits to be made before completing the requisite performance evaluation documents and closing out the assignment on each teacher. The answer for the minimum number of visits, the minimum length of each visit, and maximum spacing between visits is almost always found in the union agreement or district policies. Documentation of these dates and times is usually required in the final evaluation paperwork.

Despite my cajoling, my common experience with assistant principals was that they submitted their evaluation documents for my co-signature reflecting the minimum number of classroom visits required. Their usual number was three visits. My personal target number was ten visits with supplementary entries for other relevant professional interactions outside the classroom within the professional day. Examples of supplementary interactions in a teacher evaluation may include observations of the teacher regarding:

- Building supervision (halls, lunchroom, activities).

- Use of paid planning time.

- Attendance and participation at teacher meetings.

- Committee assignments.

- Parent conferences.

- Other required night activities for parents such as back-to-school night, curriculum night, or activities night.

My strongest recommendation is for more classroom visits rather than just the minimum required.

It is not my intention in this book to go into details of preferred certificated teacher performance evaluation documents, techniques, or other feedback mechanisms. Principals are required to use and submit the forms found in their building or district directives. For those principals unconstrained in this regard, I recommend looking into the writings of Madeline Hunter, Heidi Hayes Jacobs, Robert J. Marzano, or Charlotte Danielson easily found by typing their names in a search engine such as Google.

—m—

Chapter 11

UNION CONTRACTS

INTRODUCTION

You may be operating your school under the guidance and requirements of more than one union contract. Teachers, bus drivers, paraprofessionals, custodians, security personnel, lunchroom workers, tradesmen, and office workers may all be under the protection of separate union contracts. It is important to read and understand union contracts. You are frequently placed in the awkward position of knowing the details of each contract better than the employee raising an issue.

TEACHER UNION CONTRACTS

When working under the directions of a union contract, it is extremely important to follow the provisions of the sections that apply to your interactions with teachers. Teacher evaluations often occupy a substantial chapter in the contract. Failure to follow the provisions, required paperwork, formats, notices, and deadlines will likely nullify any work and time spent in the evaluation process. If you are trying to not rehire a teacher who fails to meet district standards in or out of the classroom, the burden of proof falls most often on the building principal. You must meet the requirements of the union contract or you will be rejected in your efforts and return a substandard teacher to the classroom.

The second most frequently referenced chapter of the union agreement to surface in building-level disagreements is titled "working conditions." A few of the topics often covered in this section include:

- Length of the workday.

- Duty-free lunchtime.

- Office and lounge amenities.

- Compensatory time.

- After-hours obligations.

- Parking privileges.

- Planning time.

If you naively wander into any of these provisions in the contract that teachers perceive as encroachment, you will elicit a response straightaway.

If you are unsure about the union interpretation of any section of the contract, do not hesitate to call their office and visit with their representative(s). Most union folks are more than willing to give you their advice. They will certainly let you know if they think your question violates the intent of the subsection being discussed. If things get heated or hostile, break off the conversation and contact your supervisor(s). It may save a lot of your time in the future if you check an uncertainty before hand rather than face a prolonged grievance down the road.

Classroom teachers and licensed, non-classroom, certified school personnel such as counselors, social workers, occupational therapists, physical therapists, speech teachers, and librarians are considered salaried employees. Salaried jobs historically fail to define time commitments for the compensation and benefits paid.

A general statement covering time commitments for salaried oc-cupations is usually a loosey-goosey reference to "whatever time it takes to get the job done."

One of my observations over the years is that the teaching oc-cupation walks the curious line between the rights, privileges, and obligations of traditional salaried jobs in the private sector and those of traditional hourly jobs. In the union contracts for certifi-cated and licensed personnel, hours of work and contract-days are repeatedly addressed in great detail. This somewhat unique attri-bute frequently supersedes administrator expectations regarding "after hours" responsibilities such as:

- Paper grading.

- Lesson preparations.

- Parent contacts.

- Semester grade submissions.

- Written recommendations for students' higher education applications or jobs.

- Additional teacher coursework to upgrade personal skills and content knowledge.

- Classroom preparations.

- Organizing the classroom.

OTHER UNION CONTRACTS

Employee contracts, other than teacher contracts, usually focus on working conditions. Most personnel under these contracts are considered "hourly workers." Their day is structured around the clock. They start and stop at specific times and have clearly defined "breaks" in their day. Part-time and full-time designations carry different obligations and privileges. "Overtime" for hourly workers can loom large in planning and managing building and district budgets.

A major complaint that emerges with hourly worker union contracts is the job description or lack of a job description. Who is expected to do what and by when? A custodian wants to empty only the trash bins inside the school, not the ones outside on the grounds. They believe the ones outside are the responsibility of the district maintenance people. Who is assigned to the job of putting the white chalk lines on the athletic fields adjacent to the building? Do building night custodians have to clean up the outside bleacher area and athletic fields after a Friday night football game? Does a paraprofessional have to supervise study hall? Isn't that a teacher's job? You get the idea.

—ɯ—

Chapter 12

STUDENT PUBLICATIONS

INTRODUCTION

Student publications in a public high school can present challenges to the principal. This can happen without much time to process possible consequences of the decisions to be made. My first recommendation is to have a hard copy of the board of education policies on "student publications" close at hand. Revocable and knee-jerk decisions can and should be avoided by following the policy.

Remember one key here is we're talking about the currently enrolled student in your school, not an adult, parent, former student, or non-student from the community or elsewhere. Let's review one familiar and one unfamiliar variety of student publications.

SCHOOL-SPONSORED STUDENT PUBLICATIONS

The most familiar school-sponsored student publications are the school newspaper and yearbook. These activities have a faculty sponsor who receives a stipend for after-school time spent. If the school newspaper and yearbook meet during the school day as a class, the sponsor is the teacher assigned. If you have a new sponsor for these activities, please take extra time with this person before the first day of class to review the applicable board of education policies.

Encourage the sponsor to exercise a "time out" (or safety valve—refer to Chapter One) if necessary to consult you as often as necessary regarding questionable material coming to them from students before they appear in a publication. This is a clear case of deal with it before publication or you will quadruple the time and stress you expend after the fact if there is a problem.

An example of a principal being criticized might be helpful. Keep in mind that the principal is legally considered a public figure. As such, a student publication is entitled to criticize the principal and their policies or practices. As long as the writing is not obscene, libelous, slanderous, or defamatory under the definition of law, the article may not be restricted from publication.

Too many angry and embarrassed principals have stopped such articles before publication that resulted in the principal being censured and "reversed" by a higher authority. In the extreme, this type of incident can lead to a resignation or termination.

NON-SCHOOL-SPONSORED PUBLICATIONS

Nonschool-sponsored publications, sometimes referred to as "underground newspapers," being circulated on the grounds or in the school building will raise important questions for the principal to consider. The questions of who, what, where, when, and how spring forth.

Who: Only duly enrolled students may circulate nonschool-sponsored publications on school grounds, by school busses, or in the school building. Non-students or adults may stand on non-school properties adjacent to the school or across the street to handout materials or even free bibles. They are under the jurisdiction of local (police) authorities, and a principal should not hesitate to ask that those local authorities check them out. Non-students attempting to circulate materials or handout freebees on campus, by arriving busses, or in the building should be confronted and deterred. Police presence may be needed to make your point.

What: An enrolled student may possess or distribute a non-school sponsored publication or other literature as long as it conforms to the same standards and limitations set in school board policy for school-sponsored student publications. Any publication in this category must be submitted to the building principal, usually 24 hours in advance, for approval prior to distribution. Students have access to an appeal process if the principal denies permission.

Where: The principal can reasonably regulate where the publication is distributed. Students would not have total access to the entire school campus and building for the distribution of their publication, pamphlet, or leaflet. Providing a table in a high foot-traffic area might suffice to meet this expectation.

When: The principal can reasonably regulate when the publication is distributed. Times considered least disruptive to the normal conduct of school would be selected.

How: And finally, the principal can reasonably regulate how the publication is distributed. For example, fellow students must have the right to accept or reject receiving a copy of the publication. Pushing the publication in all student lockers would not be acceptable. Placing copies on all lunch tables or library tables would also be unacceptable.

SCHOOL-SPONSORED PUBLICATION TRENDS

Technology is moving so fast that we are witnessing the loss of major newspapers across our country. Many long-running magazines have also disappeared. This trend is also affecting our school-sponsored student publications.

Interest in classic high school newspapers and yearbooks is shrinking. Two of eight high schools in my community are no longer printing a hard copy of their school-sponsored newspaper. The remaining six are operating on a thread. Both schools that shut down hard copy publication have continued with an on-line version with smaller numbers of students participating in the production. Yearbooks are remaining steady concerning interest while costs continue to rise dramatically. The fate of yearbooks hinges on students paying for higher production costs. If students resist buying, the classic high school yearbook will be substantially reduced in quality or fail.

Another attempt to continue school-sponsored publications during this down trend involves combining both newspaper and yearbook under one sponsor. Clearly high schools are in transition regarding school-sponsored publications. Rising costs, decreasing interest in classically taught journalism, and falling advertising and community sponsorship revenues are driving the downward movement.

Chapter 13

COPYING MACHINES

INTRODUCTION

The school copying machine or machines, if you are fortunate enough to have more than one, remains a cornerstone of efficiency and absolute necessity for teachers to meet their responsibilities to their students. How and when copying usage occurs varies among buildings. Who has access to school copying machines is also quite different among schools. Convenience can also be an issue with teachers. Paperless computer connections between teachers and students is on the technology horizon, but copying machines will be in use for most schools for years.

TURNAROUND TIME AND ACCESS

One of the big problems for teachers is how quickly they can get their copying needs met. There seems to be a direct correlation between turnaround time to obtain copies and access to the machine for copying. The difference revolves around who operates the machine. If only one person, usually an aide or paraprofessional, is allowed to operate the copying machine, turnaround time for a teacher to obtain their copy materials may increase dramatically.

The advantages to single operators of a copy machine include:

- Copy quality.

- Better teacher planning for copying needs.

- Machine maintenance and management that translates into up time.

- Overall efficiency.

- Copying advice expertise for teachers.

- Formal monitoring of inappropriate and unauthorized copying.

- Improved economy of paper use due to operator errors common with multiple users.

- Drop off and pickup by student aides.

Turnaround time can be improved by using a priority or triage system that runs small jobs first and large volume or specialized jobs during low-demand times of the day.

If teachers have what are known as "walk-up privileges," the only limits to immediate copy completion are waiting for anyone currently using the machine and the operational status of the machine itself. Teachers have strong feelings on the topic. Most teachers hate, yes hate, not having walk-up privileges for copying. Two problems argue against this prevailing emotion. One is the time needed for large copy runs. Frustration runs high when a teacher needs only thirty copies for an upcoming class and gets stuck behind another teacher running one hundred copies of a ten page, stapled document.

DOWN TIME AND ACCESS
(TEACHER WALK-UP PRIVILEGES)

A common problem in schools is machine breakdown. When a copying machine breaks down everyone gets angry and frustrated. There is also a direct correlation between machine breakdown and unrestricted teacher access to copying machines. The more people who operate a copying machine, the more it will stop operating properly. This problem is magnified with the more options the machine offers. If teachers exceed the machine manufacturers declaration of the copying capacity of the machine, breakdowns increase.

Copy machines with more options will break down more often than a machine with fewer options. For example, if the machine:

- Staples.

- Copies on both sides of a page.

- Offers more than one paper size.

- Can copy on thick paperboard, often called cardstock.

- Can reduce or increase the size of the copy page.

- Copies in color.

- Collates.

Schools decrease the probability of machine breakdown and, therefore, downtime by limiting machine access to only those individuals highly experienced and trained to operate complex machines.

Control, Access, and Billing

Copy machines offer the safety and convenience of punch codes for machine access. Teachers with walk-up privileges simply press their individual or department code into the machine to gain instant access. No entry code, no access.

A secondary benefit to access codes is the tracking of copying usage by person or department for building billing or budget purposes. The regular review of copy usage can be an eye opener in both the positive and negative sense.

Single-operator copy machine arrangements also have the capability of tracking usage by person or department except that the use data is entered into the copy machine or tracked separately by the staff aide or paraprofessional.

Another Access Issue

If a school allows walk-up privileges for copying machines, another point of discord and friction among teachers is student access to the machine or machines if a school has more than one. Teachers with highly trusted and competent student aides argue vehemently that the student aide should have access to make copies for them.

Teachers opposed to student access argue that privacy and confidentiality are frequently lost when student aides are allowed in the copy room spaces. In addition, an argument is made that misguided student aides are subject to misuse of the machines. For example, the student aide may use the machines for their personal needs or making copies for their friends. The machine breakdown factor can also be amplified when use access is granted to student aides.

MULTIPLE MACHINES

A primary response to problems surrounding a school depending on only one copying machine is to add more machines. In a two-story building, having a high-volume machine on each floor saves teachers time and hassle. If the machines are identical, familiarity with machine operation features will decrease down time. In the event of one machine being broken, the second machine can usually carry the copying load over the short term. Teachers can still get their work done.

Another quandary facing principals is requests for additional copy machines at various locations in the building other than in traditional "copy rooms." Four common locations that come to mind are the counseling spaces, athletic office, library, and administrative offices. Unique building layouts with isolated spaces might also generate more copy machine requests. Staff members with handicapping conditions must also be considered.

BUDGET NIGHTMARES AND LOTS OF CHOICES

Linked closely with multiple copy machines in a school are the associated costs. Considerations include:

- Lease or buy.

- Higher volume or lower volume.

- Maximum or minimum features.

- Maintenance agreement or not.

In addition, how does a school balance longevity against obsolescence in the long term? What electrical and wiring requirements

91

accompany each possible choice of a machine? Are there expertise, experience, and assistance in the district for these questions and considerations so you don't have to go it alone? Being exposed to a gaggle of copier salespeople on your own is an exercise in futility.

SERVING STUDENTS

It would be prudent and reasonable to provide your students with access to copying services within the schoolhouse. The most common mode to meet this demand is with a copy machine that accepts cash. If only coins can be used in this machine, a coin changer nearby is a must. Pay-as-you-go copy machines should not impact any school budget or in-house student activity funds.

The location of the machine or machines should accommodate access for the maximum amount of time possible during school hours of operation. Staff monitoring of the use of the machine is also paramount to prevent abuses, misuses, vandalism, and paper resupplies. Making calls for repairs should also be assigned to specific staff members.

—⁂—

Chapter 14

THE ASSISTANT PRINCIPALSHIP

INTRODUCTION

I served as an assistant principal for two years and a building principal in three public high schools totaling twenty-eight years (8, 12, 8). During those years as a principal, I worked with eighteen assistant principals. I developed ideas and philosophies about the assistant principalship that deviate in many ways from my contemporaries.

I viewed the assistant principalship as preparation for a principalship. I believed it was my responsibility to provide opportunities for each assistant to develop skills and accumulate experiences that translate and transfer to the principalship.

When I expressed this philosophy to many of the younger assistants early in their new position, they often balked at the idea and felt strongly that they had no aspirations beyond being an assistant. This position is understandable given the reality of a recent move from the classroom to the weighty responsibilities of helping run a comprehensive high school.

Assistant principals new to the position often struggle with a vision extending several years into their future. Waiting years to initiate exposure to the many facets of the job is a disservice to those individuals. I'm advocating for an early, comprehensive, and broad introduction to primary and collateral job duties and responsibilities.

I guided many assistant principals in my 28 years. Some accumulated years of experience, felt confident and comfortable in their role, and clearly had no interest or intention to move beyond the assistant principalship. I respected their position on the subject, but nevertheless I interacted with them applying my philosophy of preparation for the principalship.

RATIONALE

My rationale for this approach is founded on personal experiences and observations of the profession across states (Florida, Illinois, Colorado) and school districts. For example, what happens if a principal is suddenly and unexpectedly taken out of the job for health, family, or other emergencies, short term or long term? The students, staff, and community deserve a competent building administrator to step up to the responsibilities of the principalship in as seamless a manner as possible.

Preparing assistant principals to replace you is a duty. It should be part of your job description. Your school cannot slump into chaos or disarray in your absence because you failed to adequately prepare assistants. The work of the school cannot grind to a halt because assistant principals aren't quite sure what you would do.

Most large high schools organize assistant principal duties into one or two narrow job responsibilities, for example:

- Attendance.

- Discipline.

- Activities.

- Athletics.

- Curriculum.

- Budget.

- Teacher evaluations.

- Classified employees.

- Community affairs.

Often seniority and stress related to these job responsibilities seem inversely related. The rookies get attendance and discipline. Age and experience in the building or district leads to duties with curriculum and teacher evaluations.

REORGANIZATION OF STUDENT DISCIPLINE

So, exactly how did I organize the responsibilities and duties of assistant principals that were contrary to the majority of large high schools I observed starting in the 1960's?

Let me start with student discipline. My premise was that all assistant principals would share the task of student discipline. It was hard for me to observe one person being assigned to the incredible stress level associated with this task. It is overwhelming, especially when attached to daily attendance. In addition, many students go unserved on days when the volume of foot traffic in the "discipline office" is high. One serious student discipline issue could occupy an assistant principal for hours as they attempt to get some reasonable resolution and closure. Issues of other students waiting are simply not addressed.

In schools with one person performing this essential job assignment, what happens when they are ill, attend a conference, or are out of the building for whatever reason? Does attention to student discipline come to a halt? Are students told to wait in the office for the balance of the day or told to come back another day? What are your classroom teachers thinking when a student returns to class almost immediately with the message that the AP (in charge of student discipline) is not available?

By making all assistant principals responsible for student discipline these shortcomings are diminished or eliminated. Let's say a building has three assistant principals. One organizational plan has AP #1 designated as the primary responder for student discipline on Monday and Tuesday or any two days of the week. On those same two days, AP #2 is designated as the secondary responder for student discipline if AP #1 gets bogged down. And yes, AP #3 is assigned as tertiary responder if #1 and #2 are really overloaded. Should all three assistant principals be pressed into service on a really bad day, the principal must step up to the plate as the fourth responder.

This plan calls for AP #2 to be designated primary responder for student discipline on two other days, and of course, AP #3 has the primary job one or two other days on a rotational basis. So, all three assistant principals serve as the first, second, or third responder on any day of the week.

CONSISTENCY AND FAIRNESS

Using the narrow definition of AP assignments, some principals would answer that another AP fills in for the absent "disciplinary AP" on those rare occasions that they are not in the building. I suggest that consistency and fairness will suffer in this scenario and students know it. The fill-in AP may elect to talk with an offending student and put off discipline until the regular disciplinary AP is back in the office. Does the "wait until your dad gets home" phenomenon apply here?

The "one assistant principal has discipline" approach to building administrator organization exposes that individual to chronic exhaustion, excessive fatigue, and the most negative aspect of the school enterprise. It also opens that person to the potential shortcomings of position power, favoritism, and parental or staff influence. The "one assistant principal has discipline" system of building organization does not have the essential elements of intermittent monitoring, periodic self-correction, and internal safeguards of accountability.

All assistant principals should share this duty. They should hold regular discussions about fairness and consistency, seek better solutions for chronic offenders, and work toward the appropriate application of the discipline rules/code. These actions will attenuate the imperfections and shortcomings of the "one assistant principal has discipline" approach. This approach also emphasizes and encourages the lost art of administrative teamwork.

MITIGATING A WEAKNESS

A weakness in distributing assistant principal time, roles, and responsibilities is the potential breakdown in both fairness and consistency when applying district and school rules. It is extremely important to note that the principal must insist and monitor the assistant principals and meet with them regularly to compare notes. These meetings should discuss the topics of:

- Fairness.

- Consistency.

- Adherence to the written and published student disciplinary rules and Board of Education Policies.

Better and more creative solutions or alternatives for chronic offenders must also be part of these regular meeting times.

Students and their parents can and will detect any perceived significant differences between penalties allotted to one student and another for the "same" offense and insist on an explanation and

97

reconsideration. Not only is this their right but also an important facet of monitoring and keeping the system fair and consistent for all students.

I have found most challenges of this issue result from students or parents misrepresenting or misunderstanding the "facts" of a discipline case of another student in the school that they think is "exactly the same." Since assistant principals cannot discuss discipline cases of other students, challenges are usually met with assurances that fairness and consistency were followed. If after listening to a complaint, an assistant principal discovers that an error was made, they should make a correction for that student followed as soon as possible by a conference with fellow assistant principals and the principal.

GRADE-LEVEL ASSIGNMENTS

Some high schools assign assistant principals to specific grade levels with responsibilities for student discipline. I contend that this arrangement is replete with the same shortcomings I argued for one AP having student discipline responsibilities for an entire building. The volume of student traffic would certainly be reduced for one grade level only, but the AP is again tied to their office and unable to schedule themselves for any other duties. AP absences, classroom visits, and out-of-the-building occurrences remain as a significant negative to this approach.

I do agree that AP's assigned to specific grade levels is an improvement over one AP assigned to handle an entire school. However, many high schools do not have four AP's to allow this distribution to grades 9-12. Even two AP's taking two grades each results in both being in the waiting-for-discipline mode all day long.

A driving force for the assistant principal rotational approach stems from a common complaint of the assistant principals themselves. When assigned to student discipline as a primary responsibility, AP's express dissatisfaction over their loss of control of their day. They can't get anything else done. Collateral duties go wanting, are done haphazardly, or serve only to add to the stress of the primary job assignment.

Obtaining meaningful training and experience in any other of the areas of preparation for the principalship become unattainable pipe dreams. For me this justifiable complaint was a powerful motivator to divvy up the AP duties on a rotational basis. From a very pragmatic point of view, it is unacceptable that an assistant principal perform poorly on collateral duties in proportion to how seriously they take a primary and exclusive assignment to student discipline.

SMALL HIGH SCHOOLS

In smaller high schools with only one assistant principal, I suggest that the principal act in rotation with the AP and serve as back-up on days when the AP is the primary for student discipline. This does not necessarily mean equal distribution of the assignment to student discipline. It could be as modest a change as four days for the AP and one day as primary for the principal. Giving the AP one or more days per week to exclusively focus on collateral duties will go a long way towards fulfilling a commitment to develop skills and accumulate experiences that translate and transfer to a future principalship.

PERSONNEL EVALUATIONS

Another collateral duty germane to the discussion of duties and responsibilities of the assistant principalship is personnel evaluation. Most schools require periodic written evaluations or progress reports on all classified and certified, including both full-time and part-time, building personnel.

As I stated in my original premise, it seems counterproductive to assign one assistant principal to this daunting yet essential task. Building administrators need time in their day that they can commit in advance for classroom visits and pre- and post-classroom discussions with assigned personnel. Actualizing these commitments is vital for positive relationships with staff members.

One of the top five complaints I have fielded from classroom teachers is that they have not had classroom visits from their assigned evaluator or had previously arranged visits cancelled. Perhaps even worse, they experienced a no-show often with a lame excuse or no explanation much less an apology. Most teachers on an evaluation cycle or schedule want and welcome the experience. For announced classroom visits, most teachers prepare an exemplary lesson reflective of their best practices. A no-show or cancelation of a previously arranged classroom visit by a building administrator is not only disheartening to the teacher but also tantamount to disrespect. The administrator involved may never regain what was lost in this seemingly simple incident of a no-show or cancellation.

The important point is that assistant principals must have time in their work day that they control with unfettered confidence and assurance of compliance with commitments, especially classroom visit commitments. To have this control, AP's cannot be deterred from classroom visits by walk-in problems. Being in the tertiary position for responding to student discipline on a given day in the rotational AP schedule almost guarantees that the AP will fulfill classroom visit commitments. In fact, the principal should step up to the student discipline task should the work load for student discipline reach the third level potentially creating a cancelation or no-show predicament for an AP.

Staff evaluations and union contracts as they relate to staff evaluations are discussed at length in other sections of this book. The point being made here is that assistant principals must not only have time to visit classrooms and observe personnel in action but also be assured that they can make commitments leading to fruition.

ATHLETIC DIRECTOR

One of the assistant principals often pleading for exemption from duties attached to student discipline is the person also assigned duties as athletic director. For some historical reason that escapes me, the assistant principal in charge of athletics has often been put in an insulated position without expectations of additional duties beyond those surrounding traditional sports. I do not believe this is a defensible perspective.

I would concede that all assistant principals should have an opportunity to argue a rationale for reduced or variable time commitments to the task of student discipline. I would be open to deviation from exactly equal time commitments if such decisions emerged from one or more meetings with all building assistant principals in attendance.

For example, one arrangement of assistant principal time commitments to student discipline among three AP's produced an agreement of two days as primary responder for two of the AP's and one day as primary responder for the third AP. A working chart and schedule was written for a month incorporating first, second, and third level responders for walk-in and associated student discipline cases. The principal was listed as the fourth level responder and special advisor or consultant on an as-needed basis.

Another reason for insisting that assistant principals with duties as athletic director continue to share other traditional collateral duties assigned to other assistant principals is that significant numbers of former athletic directors become building principals. This phenomenon should not be a surprise. Athletic directors earn their stripes, pay their dues, and gain the skills and experience admired in and required of building principals. Athletic directors:

101

- Deal with angry students and parents.

- Organize and monitor many budgets.

- Create schedules of all sorts.

- Intervene in sports crises.

- Serve on many district and state-level committees.

- Purchase and manage equipment of many descriptions.

- Keep inventories.

- Plan for the future.

- Hire and evaluate sports personnel.

- Terminate coaches for cause.

- Work many nights, weekends, and summers.

Preparation of athletic directors for a principalship makes sense even if the athletic directors disagree at the time and do not project themselves into that role in the future.

ADDITIONAL COLLATERAL DUTIES

In addition to student discipline, certified personnel evaluations, and athletics, other assistant principal collateral duties may include:

- Student activities other than athletics.

- The building budget.

- Student activity fund accounting and budgets.

- Contact person for classified personnel.

- Classified personnel evaluations.

- Curricula.

- Technology.

- Community activities.

- Parent groups.

- Create daily and special "bell" schedules.

- Student classroom schedules and master scheduling.

- Liaison with counselors.

- Building committees.

- District committees.

- Student activity supervision.

- Special events planner and coordinator.

- Building and grounds usage and rentals.

- Security.

- Fund raising.

And, there may be additional assistant principal responsibilities in your setting.

Based on my biases as described in this section, I would suggest that principals find ways to rotate or otherwise expose all assistant principals to as many of the duties listed above as possible. The timetable to accomplish this objective could be as little as one school year but practicality would probably dictate more than one year.

A checklist would serve as a guide through the process. Collateral duty assignments should be openly discussed and assigned following a democratic process mutually agreed upon by the individuals involved. The full support, guidance, and problem solving abilities of the principal are mandatory for the success of this endeavor.

—◆◆◆—

Chapter 15

CURRICULUM

INTRODUCTION

One of the issues surrounding high school curriculum is getting newbies and transfer teachers up to speed on what they're assigned to teach in the pending fall and spring semesters. You have several options at your disposal. Perhaps activating all of them would be helpful to your new classroom teachers.

DEPARTMENT HEADS

Larger high schools have a system that identifies department heads, lead teachers, senior teachers, or master teachers. A typical expectation and collateral duty for these individuals is to mentor teachers new to their department or curriculum focus. First year teachers right out of college will need concentrated efforts to get them off to a great start. An experienced teacher from the same curricular content area or someone who has taught the same classes in the past should be assigned to the newbie.

The role of the principal, or assistant principal given the assignment, is to make the human connections and monitor the progress of the relationship.

DISTRICT PERSONNEL—
CURRICULUM SPECIALISTS

Many school districts have district-level personnel, often called curriculum specialists, who may be tapped for their expertise and hands-on contact with teachers new to the district in specific curriculum content areas. Language arts, math, social studies, world languages, special education, and science are content areas that typically have specialists at the district level. These professionals may make a contribution to orientating teachers new to your building or from outside the district.

If these educators don't currently offer those services, perhaps it would be time for a principal or group of principals to make such a request. Getting new teachers familiar with the local and state curriculum, resources available, and content standards is essential. Accomplishing these tasks before school starts in the fall or prior to the start of second semester for semester courses should be the goal.

A WRITTEN CURRICULUM

As trite as this might sound, issuing new teachers a written curriculum for each assigned course is an often-overlooked event. Written curricula should include:

- Outline and syllabus.

- Scope and sequence.

- Content standards.

- Goals and outcomes.

- Materials available such as texts, novels, lab supplies, art supplies, etc.

- Lessons.

- Assessments such as chapter, quarter, semester, and final exams.

If your school does not maintain an updated file on each course, you should consider such an undertaking. Make sure that everyone knows they exist and are accessible at the department level.

There is a strong motivator for a standard written curriculum that outlines semester or yearlong courses. There is a need for students taking a course that has multiple sections taught by different teachers to be exposed to the same content, learning outcomes, and class experiences. Two students each taking the same biology course from different teachers should cover the same material, perform the same lab experiments, use the same book, and probably take the same final course exams. It just seems odd that the opposite can and does occur. In the absence of any guidelines or agreements among teachers on course content and instruction, how can a principal justify students receiving a different syllabus in the "same" biology course because instructors have different interests, background, skills, and experiences?

CONTROVERSIAL COURSES

Perennially controversial courses or courses with potentially controversial content or sections should not be assigned to a teacher new to the building. However, if such an assignment is unavoidable, the teacher or teachers involved should receive special attention from the principal. Dialogue should occur before the start of the semester.

Specific instructions should be provided to the teacher regarding past student objections arising in the classroom. This should also hold true for past concerns from direct contacts by parents.

Prudent instructions to the teacher should include a safety valve to allow the teacher to temporally sidestep serious objections and avoid an unnecessary and a potentially explosive escalation in the classroom.

For example, as the classroom teacher is assigning the next book to the class for required reading, one student states openly and emphatically in front of the whole class that s/he will not read the book. The student may or may not state a reason. A well-placed safety valve (discussed in Chapter One) here will allow the teacher to refocus the class and address the "volatile" student's concern at an appropriate time and place.

Parent complaints should be channeled to the principal. The teacher should not be expected to take on parents or a community group that have objections, real or perceived, to all or parts of an approved school course of instruction.

REQUIRED READINGS

Some teachers get very intense about expecting every student to complete certain required readings or assignment for a course they teach. Rather than engage in combat over this issue, I suggest that reasonable objections be met with acceptable alternative books or assignments that satisfy the targeted content standard or course objective(s). The time, effort, and stress involved in attempting to force a specific requirement are generally a waste of energy.

Alternatives are often necessary for special education students in class or those students with objections based on religious beliefs. Therefore, it is not a huge deviation to have the classroom teacher hold acceptable alternatives in reserve and avoid hostilities when inevitable objections arise.

DEVIATIONS FROM THE PRESCRIBED CURRICULUM

Deviations from the approved and prescribed curriculum can take several forms. The principal's response should be tailored to the nature of the deviation.

An interesting problem arises when a classroom teacher injects personal or religious views into the curriculum. For example, what does a principal do about a math teacher who uses extensive class time to "disprove" carbon dating because this science method is used in estimating the age of ancient artifacts well beyond 2000 years ago? This particular teacher strongly believes that the earth was "made" in biblical times and therefore carbon dating is wrong and inaccurate.

Another classroom teacher in the biological sciences refuses to teach anything about theories of evolution because of strong, personal beliefs in creationism. A third example is a classroom teacher who has the documented habit of espousing any number of personal ideas, beliefs, or causes that are totally unrelated to the content and curricular expectations for a course. Political affiliations prior to elections might be a choice in this example. Raging on about this candidate or another in a physical education or art class during assigned class time is totally inappropriate and out of line.

The principal has a few options. A first step would be to establish the facts. This is best accomplished by direct contact with the potentially offending classroom teacher. Having an assistant principal present during the conversation would be good judgment. It should be viewed as acceptable for the teacher to have someone with them in the same conversation. In strong union districts, having a representative with the teacher may be standard procedure. The teacher must have an opportunity to explain any allegations in his/her own words.

Assuming the teacher acknowledges the objectionable deviations from the prescribed curriculum, the principal should issue clear verbal instructions and expectations to correct the situation. A written confirmation should follow to be hand delivered to the teacher the next work day. In-class monitoring should be part of the corrective prescription. Most teachers will respond positively and make the necessary adjustments to refocus all class instructional time as deemed appropriate.

There are cases where the teacher hunkers down, digs his/her heels in, or flatly refuses to respond to the principal's persuasion. The principal must complete the initial meeting with professionalism and as soon as possible contact superiors for assistance. The head of personnel for the district is a good first contact.

THE COURSE SELECTION PROCESS

I will highlight this section with a pet peeve. It exists in so many high schools that I fail to understand why the practice continues. The topic is how each department within the high school arrives at who teaches what courses the following school year. This planning almost always occurs in the late spring as the school prepares the course offerings and master schedule for the next school year.

In the "worst" case scenario, the department head or senior teacher in the department handles the entire event. They communicate with the school administration regarding what courses are to be offered the next year and approximately how many sections of each course will be needed. The final piece of information is the assignment of which teachers in the department will teach which courses. This all occurs with little if any communications with department colleagues or administration.

In the next variation of this activity, a select group of senior teachers in the department look at the course offerings for the next

110

year and they make their choices. This can be called selection by seniority with the most junior members of the department getting literally what's left over. This approach gets exaggerated when a department has a fair number of elective courses in the offerings. The senior members select their favorite elective courses leaving courses required for students to graduate to the more junior or rookie members of the department.

My attempt to improve this senior staff lopsided, monopoly approach centers on requiring each department to devise a democratic system of course selection that ensured fair access by all department members. I also ask that any classroom teachers who feel they did not receive a fair shake in the course selection process to please see me at their earliest convenience. I also make it clear that I will gladly supply a selection process for any department struggling with my directive for a fair, democratic process. No one ever took me up on that offer.

The process can be as simple as all department members gathering at the same time around a table with all courses and anticipated sections written on individual pieces of paper displayed on the table. Each teacher then has one pick per round of selection until all courses and sections are retrieved. The order of selection can be by seniority or by random drawing before starting the round-robin selection process.

One upshot of this democratic process will be seen in the retention of younger members of a department. Now they don't have to change schools to have a chance to teach "fun" courses or courses in their area of expertise. This can also minimize senior teachers getting a lifelong or career-long lock on certain courses in the curriculum. Another spinoff of a more democratic distribution of the courses is high levels of positive dialogue, bargaining, compromise, and attitude shifts within a department. Leveling the playing field is a wonderful equalizer in an occupation that can suffer from elitism, seniority paralysis, and faculty cliques.

A Course Selection Tweak

I have one more fine adjustment to the course selection issue that I believe generates tremendous benefits for teachers and students. In large departments, urge (or require) all teachers to select at least one section of a freshmen-level course every school year.

This keeps experienced teachers in touch with their classroom roots while helping them monitor the skills, abilities, attitudes, and interests of the newest members of the school. Losing daily touch with freshmen is counterproductive for teachers moving to the mid- and late phases of their teaching careers.

All teachers in the department should have the chance to help prepare students for more advanced courses. Positive relationships established at the freshmen level will also encourage students to elect more rigorous department courses in the coming years.

Chapter 16

GOVERNANCE

INTRODUCTION

Each fall a high school welcomes 500 to over 2000 students who have had little contact with the school for three months. Each student is given a class schedule derived from an intricate weaving of courses, teachers, spaces, needs, and requests that took countless hours and days to compile. Despite general unhappiness with one or more of the classes appearing on each student's schedule for first semester, students trudge off to start the school year with every emotion known to mankind spread among the population.

The educational enterprise is not manufacturing widgets. Schools are responsible for human beings. High schools in America are charged with positively influencing the physical, social, emotional, and intellectual growth of students aged 14 to 18 with a few less than age 14 and a few more older than 18. One of the biggest and most central questions regarding the high school principalship is: How does one govern such a large, constantly changing, and complex organization?

THE FACULTY AND STAFF

The primary resource given to a principal to meet the needs and expectations of the students, parents, and community are the employees hired by the board of education. Faculty members and many classified staff members are the folks who have direct and daily contact with the students. The principal must influence and work with the faculty and staff to accomplish the goals and multiple expectations for positive growth. The larger the school, the more difficult and challenging these tasks become.

The faculty of most high schools is composed of first-year teachers as well as teachers with thirty years in the classroom. Most of the experienced teachers have worked under the supervision of several principals. Their attitudes towards and experiences with previous principals rank from excellent to good riddance. Some faculties remain quite stable over years and others have experienced huge annual turnovers.

Faculty and staff characteristics, profiles, and demographics have a bearing on the governance of the individual school building. The board of education, superintendent, or union agreement may dictate some aspects of building governance. For example, certain parent groups, a grievance committee, or a variety of faculty committees may be required in each school in the district. Principals usually have discretionary authority to create additional forms of building governance to fill gaps or voids. How does a principal new to a building take all of these contributing factors and characteristics into consideration when assessing and reflecting on an appropriate and necessary governance plan?

ASSESSING THE CURRENT SITUATION

A first step in reviewing and planning building governance is to list and understand what currently exists. Noting the objectives of each committee and group, the membership, and impact on the school is very helpful in grasping a picture of present governance. Talking to a member or two of each governance group and committee should solidify impressions. Interviewing faculty members not serving on any of the groups can also provide valuable insights.

When reviewing and summarizing initial assessments, try to determine the existing power and influence distributions. Look at the quality and quantity of the existing groups and resolve possible gaps and unmet needs. This is a good time to review and integrate thinking about the demographics of the school and constituent groups.

Any changes in school governance being considered should include notations about the estimated speed needed for implementation in the short or long term. A plan for feedback and accountability for each anticipated change would also be prudent. Thoughts about dissolving or replacing any existing building group or committee should be discreetly tested with trusted individuals before moving ahead. Take care not to drop any group required by the district or union agreements.

MAINTAINING OR CHANGING GOVERNANCE GROUPS/PLANS

If your assessment finds high functioning groups with appropriate representation, you may only need to determine which groups warrant or demand your time and which groups you might delegate to assistant principals. If your assessment suggests changes are needed, determine which group you approach first with your plans.

Suggestions for modest changes might go very quickly with little resistance. Members may not only be receptive to the changes but also relieved that you have brought them to the table. If you have a plan and rationale for even more radical changes, members may listen and give you latitude especially during the grace period or infamous "honeymoon" granted most new principals. If your predecessor was fired or removed for cause, you have the most opportunity for innovation and change. If your predecessor retired after years of service to the building and was genuinely loved and admired by all, you will have serious difficulties making any changes. (Perhaps no changes are needed or warranted.)

When approaching changes in building governance, you should reflect on the personal style you have at your command to influence change. I highly recommend against using position power. Yes, you are the principal, and yes, you have the authority, and yes, you can be the "decider." But, short-term results pale in comparison to what can be accomplished using personal power.

Your persona is critical to your success and ability to get as close as you can to the primary objectives and directives of the school. Use and express your strengths. Supplement and minimize your weaknesses.

If egocentrism and narcissism have space in your personality, those around you will patronize you. You will constantly have to resort to position power and bullying to get things done. Genuine, enduring achievement of building goals and success will be left to others in the institution. You will be isolated and distant from the people doing the work of the school. (One colleague editor told me: "I doubt seriously that principals who behave this way will understand this paragraph.")

—⁕—

THE SINGLE HIGH SCHOOL DISTRICT VS. DISTRICTS WITH MULTIPLE HIGH SCHOOLS

INTRODUCTION

This is a quick observation for individuals entering high school administration for the first time or for experienced high school administrators looking to change school districts after their first principalship. I had the experience of working at the building administrator level, one as assistant principal and one as principal, in two districts each with a single high school and two principalships in a district with eight high schools.

There is a significant difference between being a building administrator in a school district with only one high school when compared with working in a district with two or more high schools. I should emphasize that the differences are not necessarily good or bad, just different. Understanding some of the differences may allow a better job fit or match for those anticipating their first venture into high school building administration or those seeking a change in districts.

THE SINGLE HIGH SCHOOL DISTRICT

In a school district with only one high school, the high school principal has almost unlimited access to the superintendent. In many districts they are in the same building or just across the street from each other. Phone calls or personal visits are not only expected but also welcomed. Daily contact is common and comfortable if you are in good standing. Daily contact is also common and not always so comfortable if your status is tenuous.

Issues involving planning and executing the building budget, accounting needs and questions, and attention to material acquisitions and work orders get priority, prompt attention, and rapid responses. This is not to say that the high school principal is subject to smooth sailing with little resistance regarding matters of money. However, communications usually proceed at a reasonable and satisfying pace and, once the budget is approved, action on purchase orders is timely.

The principal in a single high school district is a bit lonely when it comes to collegiality with any fellow high school principals. The fulfillment of this need or desire usually comes from meetings involving same-sized high schools associated with sports activities as assigned by the state high school activities association. Principals in these groupings often meet prior to or simultaneously with the schools athletic directors' monthly meetings. While often social in nature, lots of informal questions, ideas, and networking occur at these gatherings.

Competition and questions of equity among high schools in single high school districts are obviously nonissues.

DISTRICTS WITH MULTIPLE HIGH SCHOOLS

In a school district with two or more high schools, there are more layers of administration between high school principals and the superintendent. As the number of high schools in a district increase, the number of administrators between the high school principals and the superintendent also increases. In very large school districts, principals may not have direct contact with the superintendent for months and then only superficially in social contexts.

One of the downsides of multiple high school districts is the competition for financial resources among the buildings. Capital improvement dollar requests are especially subject to the darker side of bureaucratic procedures and requirements. The amount of time and effort expended by a principal pursuing a capital improvement project increases exponentially by the number of high schools seeking the same funds.

Textbook money is often allocated on a yearly calendar that rotates purchase authorizations by subject area. For example, math textbooks used for algebra may be purchased this school year and social studies textbooks for junior-level subjects will come up the next school year.

Most large school districts have some formula used in attempting to distribute supply budgets equitably among high schools. In micromanaging, the district may also address supply budgets at the department level. For example, science may be allocated a larger supply budget than language arts based on a per pupil amount. If macromanaging is employed, the district gives a building the entire allocated supply budget as a lump sum and allows each building to determine its own internal supply budget distribution.

Equity issues among high school buildings are important but can be quite frustrating at times. For example, if one high school is given a totally new and well-equipped computer lab, it will probably have to wait years for an upgrade or replacement until each of the other high schools gets its new lab as dictated by principles of equity.

Additional frustration can occur when this same high school seeks to replace or upgrade its computers on a quick turnaround schedule. Perhaps the school wants to add yet another new lab using money supplied by a private-sector benefactor or money donated by the schools aggressive and effective parent fund-raising organization. The superintendent or school board may nix the projects because equity will not be served.

Any one or more of the other district high schools may not have an aggressive and successful fund-raising parent group. Allowing

119

one high school to add well-equipped and updated labs unabated flies in the face of fairness and applications of equity. The aggressive fund-raising high school and their parents may now feel angry, and the parents may look for alternative schools.

Another interesting issue of equity can arise if a school serving a wealthier section of the school district wants to use parent-raised funds to retain or hire teachers, aides, or paraprofessionals, especially during times of district budget reductions. Staffing ratios among schools in a large district are often sacrosanct. A school board will not allow a "maverick" high school to use private sector funding to improve or upset these ratios. In addition, the board of education has exclusive rights to hire and fire personnel. Neither building personnel nor parent groups can usurp this legal authority.

If a principal wants, needs, and enjoys frequent formal contacts with other building principals, the multi-high school district fills the bill. Most large districts schedule one or two required meetings a month for principals. An administrator assigned to supervise high schools usually conducts the meetings and sets much of the agenda. Frequently a succession of district-level personnel wanting or needing to address high school principals are cycled through these meetings. A half-day meeting, with or without lunch included, is not an unusual time commitment for this regular event.

Chapter 18

STUDENT ACTIVITY FUND

INTRODUCTION

One of the unfortunate downfalls for a few principals appearing in the news over the past decades revolves around the high school activity fund. This is an internally managed and monitored cash accounting system that is not part of the building allocations from the school district for salaries, supplies, and equipment. The student fund collects and disburses monies from clubs, student fundraisers, and class activities. Cash accounting is the primary responsibility of the student fund.

Each high school has an employee who's part-time or full-time job is to act as treasurer for the student fund. For example, a group of students hold a weekend car wash on campus or in the community, and the cash collected should be deposited in their student fund account at the school. So, what could possibly go wrong with this system?

This is not a book or chapter to present accounting systems for principals. The purpose of this chapter is to point out that the student fund can be an Achilles heel for the principal and has a high potential for a path to job loss. In the order of importance of the items in the principal's job description, managing the student fund is usually near the bottom. However, it should be nearer to the top. The principal must spend enough time on reviewing the mechanics of the student fund and restructuring it, if necessary, to close as many loopholes and other weaknesses as possible.

Cash Abuse and Loss

Anytime staff or students collect cash for selling anything at school as a fundraiser or by students circulating door-to-door in the community, the possibility of loss, theft, under reporting, and other abuses are very real. Any high school principal can describe unfortunate experiences that led to time consuming research and interviews when abuses have come to light. Tracking cash exchanges for goods or services in a teenage environment is an exercise in futility.

In the ideal setting, the principal has faculty members or other employees who connect directly with their students for some fundraising activity. For example, students are given a box of candy bars to sell to fellow students, community friends, or relatives. Cash collected is returned to the staff member who is expected to deposit the cash with the building treasurer. Sounds simple enough.

- What happens if candy bars are stolen from a student?

- What if a student loses cash?

- What if a student allows the product to be damaged before it is sold?

- What if a student spends the cash collected before turning it into the staff member and, perhaps, lies saying it was stolen?

- What if a student gives the product to friends and does not collect the cash?

- What if the staff member accumulates the cash collected and keeps it in a file cabinet in his/her office or classroom where it is stolen prior to being deposited with the treasurer?

- What if a staff member pays bills for the fundraiser using the cash collected and has no documentation for the transactions?

- How does a principal detect if a staff member is illegally and dishonestly siphoning cash from a fundraiser?

All these possible issues must be addressed by establishing a system to monitor student fund-raising activities.

ESTABLISHING A SYSTEM BASED UPON OPENNESS AND COMMUNICATIONS

Suggestions for oversight of a student fund include:

- Create a committee to help the principal regularly review the monthly or quarterly accounting data provided by the building student fund treasurer. Two faculty members, two students, and two parents would be a manageable group. The treasurer should also be present as needed.

- One duty of this committee is to address complaints involving the student fund and its accounts. Informational and procedural issues are addressed. Accusations of mishandling of student funds require referral to higher authorities.

- The principal can assign oversight duties to an assistant principal that includes creating and meeting with the committee.

- A student fund committee can review cash-handling procedures, questionable expenditures, and potential irregularities.

- The treasurer must issue monthly data sheets reflecting transactions of all student fund accounts. Distribution of these data sheets go to all personnel with accounts.

- The principal must request periodic advice and audits from appropriate district-level personnel regarding any uncertainties, irregularities, and legalities of the building student fund.

HANDLING CASH

Most parents, students, and staff members would be very surprised to learn how much cash moves in and out of the student fund activity accounts in the course of a week, month, and school year. It is not unusual for $100,000 to be deposited and withdrawn annually in a high school with over 1000 students.

An obvious question is: How does the principal ensure the safety of cash within the building? The answer is one or more metal safes with a night-deposit slot on the top. Cash bags and deposit information slips must be available at or near the safe(s). School personnel and parent volunteers must be held to a strict standard of depositing all cash in a cash bag, properly labeled with a deposit slip, in a school safe before departing for the day. The school treasurer will access the safe and count, record, and deposit the cash as required by district policy.

I have one quick word of advice about school safe(s). Have your district maintenance department place a substantial anchor in the wall or floor at the location of each safe. A second anchor should be added (welded) to the back or bottom of the safe with a heavy-duty chain or equivalent connecting the two anchors. The rational for this extra precaution emanates from the practices of successful thieves who simply employ a two-wheeled cart to extract a school safe for opening at another, more convenient, location off campus.

PRINCIPAL-TREASURER COMMUNICATIONS

Exceptional communications between the principal and the high school treasurer are essential to ensure proper handling of the expenditures and cash flows of the student activity accounts. The treasurer must have immediate and unimpeded direct access to the principal or his/her designee regarding concerns, questions, and red flags related to the student fund.

Identifying a questionable deposit, withdrawal, expenditure, or request for funds as soon as possible is imperative. Attempting to clean up a mess or misunderstanding after-the-fact can be time consuming, damaging, and counterproductive to the educational process.

The principal must instill in the treasurer the high need to be vigilant in the execution of his/her duties and responsibilities. Honesty, ethics, and attention to detail must be hallmarks of the treasurer's daily conduct. Parents, staff, and faculty members will quickly learn that the treasurer will not:

- Cut corners.

- Extend privileges.

- Overlook problems.

- Play favorites.

- Hesitate to seek immediate advice, as needed, from the principal.

A DISHONEST PRINCIPAL

One copy editor wrote me a note asking: "What happens if the principal, the overseer, is a crook? Just wondering. How do crooked principals get caught?"

It is true that we have all heard of dishonest principals who find ways to siphon cash from gate receipts or spend school dollars on inappropriate or personal purchases. Sometimes this criminal conduct goes on for years before detection.

I had to ponder the questions for an extended time. I assume that unscrupulous principals are identified and exposed by coworkers or parents, often anonymously to district-level personnel. Eventually, the information and suspicions reach the superintendent or board of education members who initiate an investigation into the allegations. Sometimes routine audits of building books and expenditures at the district level produce suspicions that trigger closer scrutiny and inquiries that can lead to discovery of criminal activity at a building.

When discovered and criminal activity is confirmed, termination of employment follows. For reasons that I do not understand, school districts seldom pursue criminal prosecution of corrupt principals.

—m—

Chapter 19

MORE CHANGES FOR SCHOOL IMPROVEMENT

INTRODUCTION

I would like to call attention to additional suggestions for school improvement. I like to call them innovations, but I don't know if other principals have also discovered and incorporated these ideas in their school. I hope many others have.

The school letter award and school attendance connected to graduation credit are deviations from standard practices in public high schools across America. I developed both of these programs in my last twenty years as principal to address positive school climate for both students and staff and to refocus the school on the prime objectives. Each program was fine tuned over time, so the descriptions I'll provide were tailored to the students and communities I served.

THE SCHOOL LETTER AWARD

The school letter expansion program I'm recommending incorporates school activities not always recognized with this award. We are all familiar with the well-established school chenille letter for sports. Many high schools have also added band (jazz and marching), orchestra, and choir to the list of activities that can earn the coveted and celebrated school letter. I know of high schools that have expanded the letter award program to also include: speech and debate, FBLA, DECA, cheerleading, pompons, battle bots, competitive science teams, competitive engineering teams, competitive chess teams, brain bowls, and moot court/mock trial.

A key component of these additions to the traditional sports letter is competition in various formats against other high school students and teams representing their respective schools. Individuals or teams usually go head to head to match skills, knowledge, and/or creativity. Judges are involved. Prizes are often awarded. All these activities are sanctioned and supported by their school.

The underlying argument to expand the traditional working definition of the school sports letter is inclusion. The philosophical shift in thinking about the issue at the high school level is "more is better than less." Exclusionary practices benefit the few. Inclusionary practices benefit the many. High school in the United States should be about identifying with and connecting to the school and community. What better represents that notion than the good old school letter?

For those who break out in a cold sweat at the suggestion of "equating" the football quarterback with the marching band drum major, I respond: "Get over it." Both individuals put in time, effort, and study. Both interact with and respond to adults trained and experienced in the activity. Both are judged on their proficiencies. Both operate under well-established rules of fair play and sportsmanship. Both have sacrificed, persisted, and pursued their chosen activity over months and years. Both want to "win" their competitions for themselves, their team, and their school.

The historical vision of the school letter being reserved for and awarded only to high school students engaging in strenuous physical activities must give way to a perspective that includes students who compete for their school against peers at other high schools. So, chess teams in competition with other high school chess teams must be included in the school letter award program. Get past the whoops and hollers at this analogy and think seriously about what the letter award means to the individual recipient. Is the rugged sports person really diminished in any way by a chess team member receiving a school letter for his/her competitions? What exactly are we worried about? Both need and deserve recognition from their school. Both will display their letter award with pride. Some will display the award on a sweater or jacket, others will pin the letter award on the wall in their bedroom. Both will feel the pride of the accomplishment and the connection to their school.

By the way, most schools award a student one school letter the very first time along with a metal pin identifying the activity. For example, a football pin comes with the first letter earned. Sometimes the first pin is bronze, the second award is silver, and the third and fourth are gold. Similarly, the first band award is a letter and a bronze pin spelling out "Band, or Jazz." A football player who has earned a football letter and also plays with the jazz band in competition will get only the "Jazz" pin upon earning that "letter." School superstars sometimes earn so many pins over the years (representing letters in multiple activities) to place on their chenille letter that the pins all but obliterate the letter itself.

I should emphasize that each of these activities must set their own criteria to earn the coveted school letter. The focus to earn a letter is to set appropriate targets relevant to the specific activity. The standards should be high but achievable. All team members should receive a written copy of the criteria to earn the letter at the beginning of the "season" prior to the first event. There should be provisions in the written criteria for altering the standards in the future as needed as well as a statement about special circumstances for earning a letter.

All principals have been presented with special circumstances for lettering regarding a student who was severely injured in an accident, acquired a life-threatening disease, or experienced a tragedy in their personal life during the season of the activity. The written provision in the criteria regarding special circumstances for lettering can be as simple as: "In the event of special circumstances concerning the awarding of a school letter in this activity, a written referral will be submitted to the principal requesting a review of the situation. A committee of the team coach, principal, one faculty member, and one team member will act on the referral within two working days."

I have one more pet peeve about school letter awards. As high schools evolved from letter awards for boys' sports only to include girls' sports, music programs, and others, many schools designed different chenille letters for each. Examples include:

- Girls' sports were given a smaller version of boys' letter, perhaps half sized.

- Girls' sports were given a stylized version of the boys' letter. If the boys received a block letter, the girls received a script version of the letter.

- The band was awarded a smaller letter with a dominating metallophone or chime (glockenspiel) overlaying the school letter.

- The word "band" was stitched prominently across the chenille letter.

The point is that there have been many variations of the school letter issued to teams other than male sports teams. Male sports teams retained the traditional (historical) school letter award.

It would seem the purposes of this practice were to maintain the exclusive status and recognition of boys' sports. "Separate but equal" conduct in the history of the United States was wrong, declared unacceptable, and changed. I suggest that "different (letters) but equal" is also wrong and unacceptable and should be changed. Providing all school activities with the same school letter award signifies inclusivity and contributes significantly to a more positive school climate for all. It connotes equality, acceptance, respect, and recognition that all student participants are valued and connected to their school. There is no pecking order; all are worthy and appreciated.

A Special Case: The Academic Letter

Now that I have ranted on about the value and contribution made to positive school climate when employing a single school letter award to all competitive teams in the school, I will argue a special case for awarding the same school letter award for individual academic excellence. This is obviously not a team competition against-other-high-schools situation. Every student in the school has a chance to earn an academic letter.

The following details the standards and criteria used for this award at my last high school:

1. The Award: The academic award consists of the standard block chenille school letter using the standard school colors. A bronze, mountable pin spelling out the word "Academics" and a certificate will also be included.

2. Criteria: Recipients for the award will be designated at the end of the fourth quarter each school year, except seniors. Through the fourth quarter of the current school year, 9th, 10th, and 11th grade students must achieve the following minimum cumulative grade point averages to qualify. Seniors must achieve their GPA (weighted grades are included in the GPA) after their seventh semester. There are no other criteria. (A = 4.000 grade points, weighted A = 5.000 grade points)

    a.   Seniors = 3.700

    b.   Juniors = 3.800

    c.   Sophomores = 3.900

    d.   Freshmen = 4.000

These are the minimums. No mathematical rounding will be used.

3. Transfer Students: Students transferring from other high schools must complete one full semester of attendance before becoming eligible for an academic letter award. Transfer grades will be recalculated, if necessary, using current cumulative grade point average criteria.

4. Awards Ceremony: Academic letter awards will be given annually to qualified students at a fall ceremony. Graduating seniors will have special arrangements for a ceremony (usually at the spring senior awards assembly).

5. Eligibility: All students enrolled for more than one semester are eligible to compete for the academic letter award. This includes students in special education and other special programs.

6. Alterations to the Program: The Academic Letter Award Program may be altered/modified by a committee composed of the principal, a minimum of four high school faculty members, and a minimum of three enrolled students. Recommendations for changes in the program may be made through appropriate means by anyone at any time during the school year.

STUDENT ATTENDANCE

One of the most frustrating and elusive prime objectives of the high school is regular and daily classroom attendance. The work of the school is hampered when students fail to attend every class every day. Excused absences as well as unexcused absences, affect:

• The graduation rate.

• The dropout rate.

- The average daily attendance.

- Credit accumulation for graduation.

- Movement from one grade to the next.

- The rate of failure ("F" grades) in all classes.

- Costs associated with re-teaching students for subjects failed.

- Costs associated with administrator, counselor, and secretary time devoted to unexcused absences.

- Negative school climate.

- Participation in extracurricular activities.

- Student connections to the school.

- Classroom teacher frustration and effectiveness.

- Percent of the student body pursuing higher education.

- Student eligibility for post graduation financial support.

- Community attitudes towards the school and its students.

- Community support for the school.

As the CBA, Chief Building Administrator, the principal is challenged, in fact, required to address each of the items listed above. Getting students to every class every day so that classroom teachers can ply their trade are both an administrative task and responsibility.

In my last student handbook, I contributed to the section on attendance policies and procedures writing: Regular attendance is critical to success in school. This is achieved by a three-pronged effort from students, parents, and school personnel. The ultimate responsibility for attending class lies with the student. Students who are frequently absent from classes place themselves at risk of not earning credits. Excessive absences cause loss of classroom instructional time and help, and in most cases, those advantages are very difficult to regain. Many students who miss classes find it difficult to catch up, even with extra tutoring and assistance from their parents and teachers. Students cannot achieve their potential if they are not in class. Excessive absences from school or classes may cause problems such as:

- Less opportunity to develop study skills.

- Loss of educational opportunities.

- Loss of financial support to the educational programs.

- Loss of eligibility for athletics and other extracurricular programming.

- Lowered grade point average.

- Loss of class credit.

- Poor self-discipline.

- Fewer reviews for class exams.

- Lower opportunity to continue education after high school.

To address these issues and concerns, I introduced a rather "radical" shift in thinking about student attendance.

DISCONNECTING ATTENDANCE FROM CLASS GRADES

Historically, teachers dealt with excessive student absences by attaching them to the student's class grade. Missing class, missing class assignments, and missing class exams resulted in a lower class grade at the end of the term. Make-up work was a burden for both student and teacher. The student (and parent) became frustrated when they argued that they generated quality class work when they were present.

Student arguments resonated in my head. "I know this stuff, why do I have to be here every day?" Also, "My son/daughter does excellent work when they are in class. Even the teacher says so. How can the teacher lower their grade if they do excellent work?" The teachers had no alternative to address poor class attendance, excused or unexcused. Lowering the class grade was the standard response.

I cannot recall the epiphany (a moment of sudden revelation or insight) that hit me one day to break the cycle of complaints that linked class attendance to class grades. Disconnect student class attendance from the issuance of class term grades.

CONNECTING ATTENDANCE TO COURSE CREDIT

The radical idea introduced was to connect class attendance to the credits earned for the course. Class grades would be issued based on the quality and quantity of work generated by the student.

If the school uses a credit system that awards five credits for a semester course, a student could theoretically earn an "A" for from one to all five credits. The school commits to a system of parental and student notification of unacceptable school attendance after which the student will lose course credit for continued absences.

The "attendance hearing" is conducted at the school in a timely manner by an assistant principal with a parent and the student present. The parent and student have a chance to discuss and explain any extenuating issues surrounding the student's attendance record. The AP listens, renders a decision, and has the parent and student sign and date an innocuous document indicating that they understand the consequences (loss of course credit) for continued attendance problems.

I won't go into the detail of the responsibilities and procedures of the school to notify all parents and students regarding the attendance policy. Suffice it to say that everyone gets a written copy of the student handbook that contains the information. Careful monitoring of the plan by the principal is essential for its success. The "volume" of violators of this policy will dictate the amount of time and number of people that must be assigned to execute the directives especially during the first time it is introduced at a school.

If a school becomes interested in making the changes suggested above, I would add that simultaneously moving to a closed or modified closed campus as described in an earlier chapter, would greatly enhance regular and consistent class attendance. If students attend class as expected because leaving campus is not an option, the impact of linking attendance and course credit becomes much less of an issue for the majority of students. Chronic attendance violators are therefore highlighted and receive encouragement and support to correct their counterproductive conduct.

A WORD ON SEAT TIME

I have a comment that supplements the conversion and focus of class attendance from grades to course credit as tool for school improvement. As a public school administrator in a high functioning school district loaded with high functioning parents, I was frequently confronted with the concept of seat time.

I found myself essentially apologizing over the years for insisting that all high school students attend all assigned classes everyday. I stopped apologizing when it dawned on me that that's what we do. Public schools do seat time. Parents and other taxpayers pay for seat time. That's how we differ from correspondence courses, on-line schooling, home schooling, the GED, proficiency exams, etc.

We value and reward seat time. We affirm that the interaction of the student with the teacher and the interactions among students in the class are the heart of a public school education. Done well, there are no substitutes for these events.

Sometimes the term "socialization" is also thrown about as an explanation of the need for seat time. In the presence of and with the guidance of a trained and experienced adult, students learn to:

- Form a team.

- Work independently.

- Assert one's self at appropriate times and places and in appropriate ways.

- Follow directions.

- Seek assistance and explanations.

- Act appropriately within a variety of class settings.

- Exhibit self-control.

- Work with and around others.

- Meet deadlines.

- Use appropriate language in various class settings.

- Observe how others address and solve problems.

- Discern and appreciate differences among the genders.

- Develop and practice critical social skills.

So, in summary, principals need to stop rationalizing and apologizing for seat time in the public schools and reassert the critical need for students to attend every class everyday.

I hasten to state that nothing is wrong with non-seat time educational settings or pursuits. It's just that they're fundamentally different from what we do in the public schools. The two experiences produce different results and each has merits. Not good, not bad, just different. If parents and students don't want, need, or appreciate the benefits connoted by seat time, there are alternatives available.

—∭—

Chapter 20

A Model to Address Principal Responsibilities

Introduction

This book has been about presenting information seldom covered in any graduate course that prepares individuals for a school principalship. It has dealt with the practical and applied elements of public school experiences. I don't want to leave the reader with the impression that studying the theoretical and reviewing the research are a waste of one's time and efforts. It would be hypocritical to wander too far from my graduate school roots. To that end, I will briefly present one research model that principals could, perhaps should, consider when viewing their responsibilities to enhance student esteem and self-actualization.

The Maslow Model

Many of you may be familiar with the writings of Abraham Maslow. His famous 1954 book, *Motivation and Personality*, Harper and Row, New York, expressed his theory of a hierarchy of human needs represented as a pyramid. The more basic human needs are at the bottom of the pyramid followed by higher human needs as one moves "up" the pyramid. An underlying principle of the pyramid illustration is that to move up in the pyramid the layers or needs underneath each level must remain relatively satisfied.

As an example, level one human physiological needs such as air, water, food, clothing, and shelter must remain relatively satisfied to allow the individual to move to the second level that includes the human needs for safety and security.

Once the first two levels of the pyramid remain stable, satisfied, and fulfilled, the third level in the needs pyramid involves social needs and feelings of belonging. Feelings of acceptance and belonging coming from small or large social groups are part of level three.

THE SCHOOL MODEL

If a parallel of the needs described above is created and applied to schoolchildren, it is immediately apparent that school personnel have a responsibility to pay attention to the model. Different levels of schooling (elementary, middle, and high) would approach the model differently, but the underlying principles are fundamental and sound. I will focus on the high school.

At level one, the question arises: Are students arriving at the schoolhouse door hungry, ill clothed, and/or homeless? If so, they are probably not ready to engage in higher-level tasks such as learning math, science, or social studies.

Moving to level two:

- Is the school a safe place, both literally and figuratively?

- Do the bathrooms operate properly and supply privacy?

- Do student lockers properly secure personal belongings?

- Are heating and ventilation adequate and operational in all school spaces?

- Are furniture and other school equipment safe and operated with required safety precautions?

- Do school doors and windows operate properly?

- Is there an absence of real threats from outside the school, such as non-school intruders?

- Is a visitor's policy observed and properly enforced?

- Is there a real threat of violence inside the school?

- Does a student encounter unnecessary obstacles when moving from one class to another?

At level three:

- Are students scared, bullied, or subject to criticism and ridicule?

- Do they feel accepted by the faculty and fellow students?

- Do they feel like they belong in the school?

- Does anyone talk to them or greet them as they move about the school?

- Are students called by name?

- Do they have friends?

To have the opportunity to address student esteem and self-actualization, the Maslow model applied to a school setting suggests that the principal, faculty, and staff would do well to monitor and nurture the first three levels. Keep in mind that student esteem in this model includes: self-esteem, confidence, achievement, respect of others, and respect by others.

A subtle but extremely important feature or element in this model should remind principals that the loss or deterioration of a given level collapses the levels above. This tells us, for example, that moving students in our school to achieve esteem will be significantly hampered if the school is inundated with real or perceived negative safety issues.

FAILURE TO THRIVE

In many schools, small or large, numbers of students fail to thrive despite the rich environment provided, exposure to a highly motivated and skilled faculty, and the presence of a comprehensive curriculum and extensive co-curricular program. The Maslow model applied to a school raises the very real possibilities that the goals of the school, the prime objectives if you will, are not being met as a result of factors in levels one, two, and three not being adequately addressed.

Due to the complexity of the human being and the individual's ability to hide factors listed in the first three levels of the model, school personnel must double their efforts to uncover and satisfactorily address deficits. At the younger grade levels, students are probably not conscious of the operation of these factors. In the higher grades, students have become more aware of social cues. They can become victims of accumulated negative experiences described for levels one, two, and three.

In high achieving schools with thriving student populations, the number and percent of students under the "failure to thrive" umbrella may be small and therefore, require a different approach than a low achieving school with a majority of the student population carrying this label. In either case, the faculty should be charged with developing appropriate plans to alter the circumstances hindering student progress towards the universal educational goals and objectives for all students.

Factors to Be Reviewed and Reconsidered

In several chapters in this book, factors affecting Maslow's levels one, two, and three are addressed for high schools. Examples include:

- School safety.
- Closed campus.
- Extracurricular activities.
- School climate.
- Hazing.
- Student lockers.

Maslow's model applied to a school would have us believe that the more completely we address the physiological, safety, and belonging needs of our students, the more likely we will be able to achieve the desirable positive attributes of high esteem and self-actualization for the greatest number of students. My personal experiences on the staff of five high schools over several decades in multiple states would validate this assertion.

—⁓—

ADDENDUM: OPENING A NEW HIGH SCHOOL

INTRODUCTION

It is a very rare opportunity for a principal to have the privilege to open a new "expansion" high school. An expansion high school is one that is being built to accommodate increasing student enrollments that cannot be absorbed by the district's existing school(s). One of the considerations, usually made by the board of education, is what grade levels should occupy the new facility in year one, two, etc. As principal you will have input.

I opened a new, large, comprehensive high school in the fall of 1998 with grades 9 and 10. In the course of the first year of operation, I met with four other high school principals who also opened a new expansion high school in their district in the same state. The experiences we encountered and the notes we compared were uncanny.

All five principals, each with years and years of building experience in their respective districts, reported that the unacceptable student conduct and daily breaches of decorum observed were especially baffling. The shinny new and well-equipped high schools were being systematically damaged and vandalized on a daily basis.

UNEXPECTED CONDUCT

Examples of the unexpected student conduct we observed and experienced included:

- Graffiti appeared on walls, student lockers, and in student bathrooms.

- Holes were punched in sheet rock between wall studs in hall areas.

- Walls and painted areas were scratched and damaged.

- Room numbers, teacher nameplates at room entrances, and hall directional signage were removed (stolen).

- Damage and vandalism to computers and printers was common.

- Handfuls of pea gravel taken from newly landscaped areas just outside the entry doors were brought inside the building and thrown about.

- Newly planted saplings on campus were striped of their branches.

- Door closers were broken off their anchor points.

- Holes were punched in overhead ceiling tiles.

- Doors on student hall lockers were bent rendering them inoperable.

- Trash was strewn about well beyond reasonable limits.

THE ABSENCE OF UPPER CLASSMEN

As the five veteran principals tasked with opening new expansion high schools put their heads together to discuss the unexpected and perplexing negative student conduct of our ninth and tenth graders, we focused on the most obvious difference between our new school and our collective experiences with our previous high schools: the absence of upper classmen. Under a cloud of guilt and naivety, the five principals concluded they failed to predict and address the effects on younger students navigating their daily school activities without the presence, guidance, and influence of upper-classmen. We significantly underestimated the moderating and modeling affects of juniors and seniors.

OPENING A NEW "EXPANSION" SCHOOL WITH GRADES 9 AND 10

The board of education has financial, political, and other considerations to review prior to establishing the grade levels that will be served by a new district high school opening to accommodate increases in student enrollments. If the board decides to open the new expansion high school with grades 9 and 10, two different situations arise. Ninth graders will enter the new high school without prior experiences in a high school. The transition will be "normal." That is, all previously established transition activities, expectations, and procedures from middle school (or junior high) to high school are in place with parents and school personnel well acquainted with how to proceed.

However, incoming tenth graders were ninth graders at another high school, usually in the same district. They had friends. They knew the school and the daily routine. They joined clubs and sports teams. They purchased and donned school clothing and other memorabilia. They identified with their school. They looked forward to returning to their school as sophomores in the fall.

Entering 10th graders were told in the spring by the school district or their parents (maybe they had a choice to stay or go to the new high school) that they would be attending the brand spanking new high school across town in the fall. If they were happy with their current school enrollment, they began to resent the change.

Fourteen and fifteen year old high school students don't always take to change of this magnitude with grace and immediate acceptance. The idea of starting all over again at a new high school is very disconcerting.

Students welcoming the change to a new high school present a different challenge for school principals.

- Did they fail to bond with friends and faculty at their other school?

- Did they have bad, unfortunate experiences during their first year as freshmen?

- Do they "hate" their current school?

- Are their parents forcing them to change schools against their will?

- Were these students given a choice to stay or attend the new school?

- What baggage will these tenth graders bring from their ninth grade year?

New surroundings, new rules, new faculty, new routines, and new everything can be daunting rather than exciting and challenging like many adults (including school people) would anticipate.

OPEN WITH NINTH GRADE ONLY

In a school district with the need to add another (expansion) high school, I highly recommend starting the school with ninth grade only and adding a grade per year until the full complement is attained. Shaping and guiding incoming eighth graders with no previous experiences in high school is a much more manageable task for school personnel.

As outlined above, forcing students in selected grade levels out of their "old" high school into the new high school is fraught with problems. The absence of upperclassmen for these students is counterproductive and may actually encourage unexpected and sometimes bizarre behaviors. Suffering through damage and vandalism can take years to correct. A negative reputation established in the first year can haunt a high school as it attempts to achieve the excellence established and expected of all the existing district high schools.

CLOSE THE OLD AND OPEN THE NEW HIGH SCHOOL

Contrary to the scenario described above, school districts usually avoid negative experiences by totally closing an aging high school and moving everyone, students and staff, to the new high school. The circumstances are different in that the student dynamics among and between grade levels did not change. The juniors and seniors continued to model appropriate behaviors for the underclassmen. No one had to leave their friends at the old school to attend the new school. Relationships with faculty and staff members remained in place. For the most part programs, rules, routines, and expectations did not change significantly. There were no haves and have-nots. No new school colors, mascots, or names. Everyone got to experience the new everything. The changes are positive with very few negatives.

—⁓—

CPSIA information can be obtained at www.ICGtesting.com
Printed in the USA
LVOW04s1849110115

422398LV00031B/1632/P